Longman Study Texts

The Merchant of Venice

Longman Study Texts   **General editor: Richard Adams**

Titles in the series:

William Shakespeare

The Merchant of Venice

edited by
Gāmini and Fenella Salgādo

with a personal essay by
David Suchet

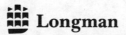
Longman

LONGMAN GROUP LIMITED
Longman House
Burnt Mill, Harlow, Essex CM20 2JE, England

First published 1986
ISBN 0 582 33193 5

Set in 10/12 pt Baskerville, Linotron 202

Produced by Longman Group (F.E.) Limited
Printed in Hong Kong

We are grateful to the following for permission to reproduce
photographs: Joe Cocks Studio, page 267; Donald Cooper,
pages xvi, 263, 264, 265, 266, 268 and 269.

Contents

Talking about Shylock – a personal essay

*by David Suchet**

Getting to know Shakespeare

My relationship with Shakespeare has developed over the years. You know how our feelings about people change? We meet someone to whom at first we take an instinctive dislike, then – after a while – we find there's something about them. In the end, we become the best of friends.

My first introduction to Shakespeare at school left me pretty cold. Like so many students who meet him for the first time at the age of fourteen or fifteen, I couldn't see very much in him. Any enjoyment I might have got out of reading the plays in class was overshadowed by all those notes and by technical jargon like 'iambic pentameter' or 'final couplets'. However much enthusiasm the teacher brought to our classes, it just was not powerful enough to infect me. I yawned my way through that year, indifference at first sight! So it's perhaps a little strange that I'm able to recall what we studied: we did 'the Henries' – *Henry IV Part 1* and *Part 2* – and *Macbeth* for 'A' level. Now the only reason I got to know *Macbeth* (and in fact passed the exam) was that it also happened to be the school play that year. I was cast as Macbeth and I not only learned my own part thoroughly, but I also took on board most of what the other characters have to say. It was only from that time of close involvement with the play – from the inside, if you like, as an actor, rather than from the outside as an exam

* Based on a conversation with Richard Adams.

candidate – that my real interest in Shakespeare started to grow. I was about seventeen: it came to me as I stood there on the stage that not only were the audience paying close attention to what I was saying and doing, they were also actually enjoying it. And it was *Shakespeare*! And I was enjoying it too! That was the beginning.

I never really wanted to be a classical actor – the type that makes his or her career performing the acknowledged masterpieces of the stage, including Shakespeare. I started off with great dreams of being in popular series on television and things like that. I had no idea that my career was ever going to move – as it has done – into the classics. I spent several years as a young actor in rep., which meant months on end rehearsing and presenting plays of every conceivable kind in little theatres up and down the country. And there I came across friend Shakespeare again: because in every repertory theatre it's pretty well compulsory that the company puts on one Shakespeare play each year – usually because it's a set text for 'O' level and it guarantees a few full houses and captive audiences from the local schools. It was on one of these occasions that I was seen in a Shakespeare play by one of the casting directors of the Royal Shakespeare Company out talent-spotting and I was invited to audition to become a member of the RSC.

You could say that my relationship with Shakespeare looked at that stage as if it was going to turn into something wild and passionate: but it didn't, because although I passed the audition and was offered a place in this – the most prestigious Shakespeare company in the world – I actually turned it down. I did so because I suddenly realized that, although I was by now very fond of the plays, I couldn't see myself fulfilling a two-year contract doing *nothing but* Shakespeare. That was one reason. The other was that I was offered a contract in which I was to 'play as cast' – not being invited to play any particular roles (even small ones) in advance, but having to take whatever was available when the director started to pull the production together. This might mean that I was cast in walk-on parts, just carrying a spear, for two whole years – and that I certainly didn't want after having been moderately successful in rep. for some time. Well, to give them their due, the powers-that-be at the RSC didn't leave it at that. The second time they approached me they offered me specific roles – Tybalt in *Romeo and Juliet* and Oliver in *As You Like It*, with the rest of the contract 'play as cast'. I consulted a number of friends whose opinions I value and they advised me to take up the offer. The roles named certainly weren't great ones, but they were a fair start. So I said yes. That was in the summer of 1973 – my relationship with Shakespeare was developing quite nicely!

At that point, however, I had the most extraordinary piece of good fortune – though it was regrettably at someone else's expense. As well as being cast as Tybalt and Oliver in that first season with the RSC, I was also understudying two rather more meaty roles in the plays in question – Mercutio in *Romeo and Juliet* and Orlando in *As You Like It* – both of which were being played by a very fine actor called Bernard Lloyd. Unfortunately, not long after *Romeo* had opened, Bernard sustained a very severe back injury and had to withdraw from both plays. So I found myself, in my first season at Stratford, appearing in two leading Shakespearean roles. It was a big jump in my career. And it meant that my relationship with Shakespeare was quickly to become even more intimate than it had been in the past. You see, if I *had* accepted that 'play as cast' contract and been given – perhaps – the parts of the odd messenger or soldier or attendant lord, it would have been all too easy for me to remain aloof from the action in those sections of the play with which I was not directly involved. But playing Mercutio and Orlando, I not only had to master the lines and characters and their relationships with other characters, I also had to dig deep into the language of the plays. And I don't for a moment want to pretend that Shakespeare's language is any less difficult or complex for the grown-up actor than it is for the teenage school pupil. It dawned on me at that time, as never before, that Shakespeare's language was basically designed to be spoken aloud, to be performed. Once I learned as an actor how to lift those words off the page, I realized that there is no need for any of the plays, ever, to be a drag. They come to life, they become theatre – meaningful, exciting and full of human understanding. And on that point I have to say that to my way of thinking, of all the writers I have performed in the course of my career, Shakespeare is the one whose works most readily retain their relevance. They say as much to us in the 1980s as they did to their original audiences – and they say it just as clearly. But at the same time – and this is another aspect of Shakespeare's genius – none of those plays is black and white, none of the themes is treated in a neat, cut-and-dried fashion. *Romeo and Juliet*, for instance, is as much a play about hate as it is about love. The characters come in a wide range of subtle colourings – few (if any) are all good or all bad. They are never basic, never bland, because Shakespeare understands human nature and human situations far too well to allow them to become so.

And that adds to the excitement of preparing a role. I regularly have differences of opinion with directors and other actors over how characters should be played and stage relationships interpreted. That kind of conflict can be at the same time frustrating and rewarding. I find myself bashing my head against walls (metaphorically speaking) time and time again, but what emerges is very often a much more thoughtful view of things – often a compromise – than might otherwise have been possible. Shakespeare really lends himself to that kind of give and take. It's one of his glories. And we should be as willing to recognize the fact sometimes in the classroom as we are in the theatre.

Playing the Jew

I remember very vividly the circumstances under which I was asked to play Shylock for the RSC: they came to me with the suggestion that I take the part and I thought 'What a wonderful offer! What a splendid opportunity!' I was really deeply grateful because success in that role could do great things for my reputation and career. But I said no. And I said it for three reasons – firstly, because I felt I was too young for the part; I think the actor playing Shylock needs to have a degree of emotional maturity if he is to get beneath the skin of the character, and I wasn't sure I was ready for it. I'd already played the part before in my career, and hadn't been entirely happy. Secondly, I was simply scared: although Shylock only appears in five scenes, he dominates *The Merchant of Venice*, and people go to see the play in order to witness *his* triumph, *his* despair, *his* defeat rather in the way they buy tickets for *Hamlet* in order to go with the prince through the agonies of coping with the task of avenging his father's murder. Just as they know 'To be or not to be' by heart, so they are there following every word, every pause, every breath of 'Hath not a Jew eyes?' My third reason for initially turning down this magnificent offer was because the director, John Barton, had worked on another production of the play only a year earlier and I was worried that he might be so close to the text, having thrashed it out with another cast, that he would wish to impose his own interpretation on me and my fellow actors, and that there would be no scope for whatever ideas about the character I might be able to come up with. I was worried, in other words, that under this particular set of circumstances, there wouldn't be any room for that all-important compromise. Well, to cut a long story short, I went away and reread the play and started thinking afresh about what makes Shylock tick. And I had a long talk with John Barton in the course of which it became clear to me that he would be open to a new Shylock, a different approach to the role, and that he would – in a word – be very supportive. So I backtracked. And I'm very glad I did. It's always nice for an actor to be associated with a successful production, and – if the critics were anything to go by – our *Merchant* turned out to be something of a hit.

Well, now I had to get down to business. One of the things I like to do when I'm preparing a major Shakespearean part is to go back and find out something of the historical context in which it was written, and to see how it has been interpreted by other actors over the years. With *The Merchant of Venice*, I was very fortunate in meeting a gentleman called Bill Colman, of Iowa State University in America, whose life's passion has been to compile a complete stage history of the play – accounts of well nigh every performance that can be traced, fully documented with articles and reviews and reports. Some years back, Bill passed all this material over to me and it made invaluable reading when I was starting to think about Shylock. So, with the play open beside me, I started doing my homework. With Shylock, of course, one of the things I wanted to know about was the history of Jews in England. And the first thing that struck me was that any practising Jews who were in this country at the time Shakespeare wrote *The Merchant of Venice* were in fact living here illegally. They had been officially banned since the late twelfth century, though a number were living in London in the 1580s and 90s, having been nominally converted to Christianity for appearances' sake. However, their range of permitted business or professional activities was severely limited. There was, in fact, one major outburst of anti-Semitic feeling in the capital round about the time of the execution for treason in 1594 of Queen Elizabeth's physician, a converted Portuguese Jew called Roderigo Lopez. Indeed, up to the time that Shakespeare wrote *The Merchant of Venice* (possibly late in 1596 or early the following year), the Jew, as represented on the English stage, had had a pretty bad press. He was, quite simply, the devil – the redhaired, blackfaced figure of the morality dramas, associated with all things evil, with hell and witches and bubbling cauldrons. And what particularly fascinated me was to discover that there was another 'Jew-play' enjoying popularity in the London theatres during the last decade of the sixteenth century: Christopher Marlowe's *The Jew of Malta*, written about five or six years before *The Merchant*. Now the Jew in this play – Barabbas – is very much of the traditional type: a savage, ranting figure, who enjoys his role as persecutor of Christians, relishing every moment of the horrors he commits and dying, at the end of the play, swearing revenge and entirely unrepentant of his evil. Shylock is like Barabbas in a number of ways (and it's worth noting that Shakespeare's play was known in his own day by an alternative title, very similar to Marlowe's – *The Jew of Venice*): they both have only daughters, both are very wealthy, both hate and do their best to catch out their Christian victims, and both are in the end thwarted in their aims. But Shylock is far from being the blackhearted monster popular in the old theatre. While there is still much cruelty and evil in him, there is equally a good dose of suffering humanity. That's plainly what was new in Shakespeare's creation of the character, and it is clearly a quality that the actor playing Shylock needs to bring out. Incidentally, there's a nice little side-glance at Marlowe's play in the Trial Scene when Shylock mutters under his breath his scorn for Bassanio and Gratiano as husbands:

These be the Christian husbands! I have a daughter,
Would any of the tribe of Barabbas
Had been her husband, rather than a Christian.

I don't want for a moment to suggest that Shakespeare saw Shylock as a 'good' man – he expends a great deal of energy in the course of the play, after all, trying to trap and kill another man – and there are very few 'good' characters in Shakespeare who are allowed to get away with such a thing. However much we may sympathize with Shylock for the cruelties and indignities he suffers at the hands of the Christians, he is patently wrong to have that urge to murder. You can't take a pound of flesh from the part of a man's body closest to his heart without causing his death. It's no joke. It's a calculated act of butchery. When I first played the part of Shylock in 1970 – before I joined the RSC – it was proposed that I should be equipped with a scalpel in the Trial Scene, as a way of suggesting the cold, clinical nature of my intentions. But I reacted very strongly against the idea. I went out instead and

bought a pound of steak to help me visualize what – as Shylock
– I was aiming to do to Antonio. I had it on a plate beside
me while I was studying the play. And, you know, a pound
of steak is a heck of a lump of meat! If I was supposed to cut
off a pound of anybody's flesh I was going to need more than
a scalpel to do the job. So I ended up with a large, wicked-
looking butcher's knife. I had the same for the Stratford
production, only there the scales I took along to weigh the flesh
were rather light and delicate – robust enough for the purpose
but a reminder that I was more used to weighing coins than meat
– bankers' scales. So there I stood: the civilized, sophisticated
man of business who is possessed with an incredible and
unforgiveable bloodlust. It is worth remembering that the
event which spurs Shylock on to his revenge against Antonio
is the elopement of his daughter, Jessica. On paper, it seems
odd perhaps that anyone should react so extremely and so
murderously to such a happening. His behaviour shows us just
what a complex and unpredictable man Shylock is, even
allowing for the way the Christians seem to gang up on him.
We should remember, too, that what might seem to us to be
the needlessly vindictive attitude of the Christians towards the
Jew in this play would have been a good deal more acceptable
to Shakespeare's contemporaries. They really did believe that
Jews were damned and that when they died they would go to
hell. To them, the forced conversion of Shylock at the end of
the Trial Scene would not have been a punishment but a
means of his salvation. Another problem for modern audiences
is the sympathy and guilt we feel over the sufferings experi-
enced by Jews during the Second World War. To us, the word
ghetto suggests the horrors of the Nazi destruction of Warsaw.
But to Shakespeare and his contemporaries, it was neither
more nor less than the name of a particular quarter of Venice
where many Jews had settled and set up business. The holo-
caust has made it impossible for us – whether we be actors or
audience – ever again to feel the relationship between Shylock
and the other characters in *The Merchant of Venice* quite in the
way Shakespeare conceived it – no matter how hard we may

try. And in some ways, that is no bad thing. The play can stand a fair range of interpretation within the limits imposed by the actual text.

Shylock relishes the circumstances which bring Antonio into his power – there's no doubt about that. Antonio, normally a man who can lay his hands readily on whatever money he needs, has a cash-flow problem; and when Bassanio asks for help in financing his expedition to Belmont, he is obliged to borrow where he can. He tells Bassanio to

try what my credit can in Venice do

– to look around the business community for someone willing to advance the necessary sum on the strength of Antonio's reputation. Now Antonio and Shylock would not normally have considered doing business together: they dislike each other intensely. But Antonio is desperate to help Bassanio and Shylock sees the transaction as a way of getting power over his enemy. There is no doubt that he thoroughly enjoys that first encounter with Bassanio in Act 1, Scene 3. He plays his victim rather as a fisherman plays the fish he aims to catch. It is a situation with a good deal of humour for Shylock, and I wanted, when I played the part, to bring it out as effectively as possible. It is important for us to remember that *The Merchant of Venice* is a comedy not just in the scenes involving the Gobbos or the tricks played on their husbands by Portia and Nerissa. Even the Trial Scene – that classic cliffhanger of a courtroom drama – has a good deal of witty, almost slapstick exchange. But, going back for a moment to Act 1, Scene 3, one can't help noticing how the colour of the language changes once Antonio arrives on the scene. As Bassanio goes to greet his friend, Shylock turns to the audience and soliloquises in a much darker vein than the one he has employed with the young suitor. He confides to us that he hates Antonio not only for being a Christian but – more importantly – also because he has undercut Shylock's business transactions by lending out money free of interest. The humour returns when he next speaks to Bassanio, pretending that he is trying to work out how he can raise the cash, and, especially, in the wheedling, oily manner in which he greets his enemy.

Shylock is certainly a larger-than-life figure: that he 'took over' the play, in a manner of speaking, dominating the action and monopolizing the emotions of the audience right from the start, is borne out – as we have seen – by the fact that even in Shakespeare's own lifetime the play was sometimes known as *The Jew of Venice*. Since the Second World War – as we have also seen – the attitude of actors playing the part as well as that of audiences watching the play has been profoundly affected by the terrible suffering of the Jews under Nazi rule. Some productions have been so sympathetic towards Shylock that they have made him appear the only shining light in an otherwise corrupt and cynical world – an interpretation which is surely very far from what the playwright intended. Shylock finally leaves the stage in Act 4, Scene 1, when the play has still more than an act to run. And one of the problems of exaggerating Shylock's dramatic and emotional importance is that it makes it very difficult for the action in the scenes which follow his departure to make its proper impact. Shakespeare was too good a craftsman to miscalculate in such matters. He wanted his play to end on a happy note; he wanted to re-emphasize the controlling influence of the female characters – a theme amply developed in the Belmont scenes and at Antonio's trial; and he wanted to show that though Antonio may have come out of the business-bond with Shylock in a safe and satisfactory manner, his protégé Bassanio was going to have to watch his step in his dealings over the marriage-bond with his new wife. It is up to modern actors and directors to ensure that Shylock does not make this scene appear redundant, by maintaining as far as possible a just balance between his character and the other important elements in the play.

There have been many different interpretations of Shylock's final lines and exit in Act 4, Scene 1. My view is that Shylock is a survivor. He has taken a calculated risk, planning the judicial murder of someone he loathes, while knowing that by

David Suchet's Shylock in the RSC production of 1981 at the Aldwych.

doing so he was putting his own life in jeopardy. In spite of the fact that he failed in his objective, under Venetian law he might well have still been executed. Instead, however, his sentence is lightened and he is given – through conversion to Christianity – the chance, as Shakespeare's contemporaries would have seen it, of salvation. What is more, being a Christian gives him (as it gave in real life to the unfortunate Roderigo Lopez) social acceptability and the opportunity to enter into other businesses or professions than that of money-lending. So I don't personally go for the tense, anguished, howling kind of exit. My Shylock recognizes that he has had a lucky escape and that the accommodation is a fair one. When he leaves the stage, he knows full well that he still has a life ahead of him.

On the other hand, of course, Shakespeare pulls no punches in his portrait of Christian society – with all its humbug and materialism and singular lack of most of the Christian virtues. Look how the other characters gang up on Shylock in the Trial Scene, how Gratiano baits him, how the word 'Jew' is flung at him time and again. In spite of the fact that his identity is formally established at the start of the proceedings, he is addressed by his name only six times, as against 'Jew' twenty-two times.

So whose side was Shakespeare on? Well, as I said earlier, I don't believe any of his plays deals in black and white, providing simple answers to complex questions. The important thing is that he leaves us thinking, he gives us elbow-room for our own interpretations, audiences and performers alike. That's why I'll always be pleased to act Shakespeare, why I'm even beginning to look forward to my next Shylock!

The Merchant of Venice

The interior of the Swan Theatre in Elizabethan times.

CHARACTERS
in the play

THE DUKE OF VENICE
THE PRINCE OF MOROCCO
THE PRINCE OF ARRAGON } *suitors to Portia*
ANTONIO, *a merchant of Venice*
BASSANIO, *his friend, and a suitor to Portia*
GRATIANO
SALERIO } *friends of Antonio and Bassanio*
SOLANIO
LORENZO, *in love with Jessica*
SHYLOCK, *a Jew*
TUBAL, *a Jew, his friend*
LAUNCELOT GOBBO, *the clown of the play, Shylock's servant*
OLD GOBBO, *Launcelot's father*
LEONARDO, *Bassanio's servant*
BALTHAZAR
STEPHANO } *Portia's servants*

PORTIA, *an heiress, mistress of Belmont*
NERISSA, *her maid*
JESSICA, *Shylock's daughter*

RICH MERCHANTS OF VENICE, OFFICERS OF THE COURT
  OF JUSTICE, A GAOLER, SERVANTS, AND OTHER
  ATTENDANTS

———————

The scenes are laid in Venice, and Portia's house at Belmont.

Antonio is evidently replying to a question asked by one of his companions.

1 *in sooth:* truly.
  sad: grave, serious.
5 *I am to learn:* I cannot tell.
6 *want-wit:* one lacking understanding. Antonio's depression makes it impossible for him to understand its cause.
9 *argosies:* rich trading vessels.
  portly: swelling.
10 *signiors and rich burghers:* fine gentlemen and wealthy citizens.
11 *pageants:* decorated carnival floats.
12 *overpeer:* look down on.
15 *had I such venture forth:* if I had so much invested at sea.
17 *still:* continually.
19 *roads:* sheltered seaways, anchorage.
21 *out of doubt:* without doubt.

Question

What, according to Salerio, do the ships and the citizens have in common?

Act One

Scene one

Venice. A street.

Enter ANTONIO, SALERIO, *and* SOLANIO.

ANTONIO

    In sooth, I know not why I am so sad;
    It wearies me; you say it wearies you;
    But how I caught it, found it, or came by it,
    What stuff't is made of, whereof it is born,
    I am to learn;   5
    And such a want-wit sadness makes of me
    That I have much ado to know myself.

SALERIO

    Your mind is tossing on the ocean,
    There where your argosies with portly sail,
    Like signiors and rich burghers on the flood,   10
    Or as it were the pageants of the sea,
    Do overpeer the petty traffickers
    That curtsy to them, do them reverence,
    As they fly by them with their woven wings.

SOLANIO

    Believe me, sir, had I such venture forth,   15
    The better part of my affections would
    Be with my hopes abroad. I should be still
    Plucking the grass to know where sits the wind,
    Peering in maps for ports, and piers, and roads;
    And every object that might make me fear   20
    Misfortune to my venture out of doubt
    Would make me sad.

23 *ague:* fever.
25 *hour-glass:* a device, rather like a large egg-timer, used to measure time before clocks were in common use.
27 *Andrew:* The name of a ship which may refer to a Spanish galleon captured by the English in 1596.
    docked in sand: embedded in the sand.
28 *vailing:* lowering sails as a sign of submission and possibly a reference to taking off one's hat as a sign of respect.
29 *burial:* burial place. The ship with its topsail stuck in the sand and its hull up in the air puts Salerio in mind of a gentleman doffing his hat and bowing down to the ground in submission.
31 *bethink me straight of:* think immediately of.
32 *gentle:* noble.
35–6 *but even now . . . nothing:* passing in a moment from being valuable to being worthless.
36–8 *Shall I . . . sad?:* How can I imagine this without also imagining my sorrow if it actually happened?
38 *bechanced:* should it happen.
42 *bottom:* ship's hold.
44 *Upon:* dependent upon.
46 *fie, fie:* a dismissive expression – 'Nonsense!'

Questions

1 Lines 30–4. How does Salerio's image in these lines suggest that the ship is both splendid and vulnerable?
2 What do Salerio and Solanio think is the cause of Antonio's depression?
3 What impression of the life in Venice is given to the audience by the speeches of Solanio and Salerio?

SALERIO

           My wind cooling my broth
Would blow me to an ague when I thought
What harm a wind too great might do at sea.
I should not see the sandy hour-glass run   25
But I should think of shallows and of flats,
And see my wealthy Andrew docked in sand,
Vailing her high top lower than her ribs
To kiss her burial; should I go to church
And see the holy edifice of stone   30
And not bethink me straight of dangerous rocks,
Which touching but my gentle vessel's side
Would scatter all her spices on the stream,
Enrobe the roaring waters with my silks,
And, in a word, but even now worth this,   35
And now worth nothing? Shall I have the thought
To think on this, and shall I lack the thought
That such a thing bechanced would make me sad?
But tell not me, I know Antonio
Is sad to think upon his merchandise.   40

ANTONIO

Believe me no, I thank my fortune for it –
My ventures are not in one bottom trusted,
Nor to one place; nor is my whole estate
Upon the fortune of this present year;
Therefore my merchandise makes me not sad.   45

SOLANIO

Why then, you are in love.

ANTONIO

           Fie, fie!

SOLANIO

Not in love neither; then let us say you are sad

50 *Janus:* Roman god of entrances and exits who was depicted as facing in two different directions. One of his two faces was smiling and the other frowning.

51 *framed:* created.

52 *peep through their eyes:* with eyes screwed up in laughter.

53 *laugh . . . bagpiper:* Bagpipe music was considered to be mournful while parrots were considered to be very silly creatures.

54 *vinegar aspect:* sourfaced.

56 *Nestor:* an old Greek King who was famous for his seriousness.

52–6 Solanio is contrasting two kinds of people, those as silly as parrots who would laugh even at sad music and those who refuse to smile even when the highest authority for gravity recommends a joke as worth a laugh.

61 *prevented:* forestalled.

64 *embrace th' occasion:* take the opportunity.

66 *when shall we laugh?:* when shall we have a laugh – an amusing meeting?

67 *you grow exceeding strange:* you have become like strangers – I hardly ever see you.

68 *We'll . . . on yours:* we shall arrange our free time to suit your convenience.

Questions

Line 60. Antonio's friends are trying to talk him out of his serious mood. Melancholy – what we would now call depression – was treated by giving the afflicted person companionship, telling him jokes, and offering him drinks in order to talk him out of his indisposition.

1 What impression have you formed of the relationship between Solanio, Salerio, and Antonio after reading this part of Scene 1?

2 Look back at the opening lines of the scene. Try to compose the question asked of Antonio to which his first speech is an answer.

Because you are not merry; and 't were as easy
For you to laugh and leap, and say you are merry,
Because you are not sad. Now, by two-headed
  Janus,   50
Nature hath framed strange fellows in her time;
Some that will evermore peep through their eyes,
And laugh like parrots at a bagpiper;
And other of such vinegar aspect
That they'll not show their teeth in way of smile,   55
Though Nestor swear the jest be laughable.

Enter BASSANIO, LORENZO, *and* GRATIANO.

Here comes Bassanio, your most noble kinsman,
Gratiano, and Lorenzo. Fare ye well,
We leave you now with better company.

SALERIO
I would have stayed till I had made you merry,   60
If worthier friends had not prevented me.

ANTONIO
Your worth is very dear in my regard.
I take it your own business calls on you,
And you embrace th' occasion to depart.

SALERIO
Good morrow, my good lords.   65

BASSANIO
Good signiors both, when shall we laugh? say,
  when?
You grow exceeding strange; must it be so?

SALERIO
We'll make our leisures to attend on yours.

Exeunt SALERIO *and* SOLANIO

74–5 *You have . . . much care:* You worry too much about wordly affairs and those who do so miss out on the good things of life.

80 *With mirth . . . wrinkles come:* Let my wrinkles of old age come from good humour and laughing.

81–2 The liver and the heart were considered the vital organs specifically connected with love and strong feelings.

82 *mortifying:* killing. Gratiano would rather drink himself into good humour than kill himself through the misery of self-denial.

84 *cut in alabaster:* like a statue on a tomb.

85 *jaundice:* an illness accompanied by depression.

86 *peevish:* moody, ill-humoured.

89 *Do cream . . . pond:* form a sour expression like scum on a stagnant pool.

90 *do a wilful stillness entertain:* deliberately adopt a pose of seriousness.

91 *be dressed in an opinion:* get the reputation (of).

92 *conceit:* understanding.

93 *Sir Oracle:* An oracle was supposed to be the voice of a god uttering truths hidden from human beings.

94 Proverbially, dogs barked at people in disgrace.

Questions

1 How do Gratianio's words to Antonio suggest that his relationship with him differs from that between Solanio and Salerio and Antonio?

2 Lines 77–9. Explain Antonio's answer to Gratiano in your own words. How does it differ from the impression of himself he has given to Solanio?

3 Lines 79–86. What does Gratiano's response suggest about *his* character?

LORENZO

My Lord Bassanio, since you have found Antonio,
We two will leave you, but at dinner-time   70
I pray you have in mind where we must meet.

BASSANIO

I will not fail you.

GRATIANO

You look not well, Signior Antonio,
You have too much respect upon the world.
They lose it that do buy it with much care –   75
Believe me, you are marvellously changed.

ANTONIO

I hold the world but as the world, Gratiano,
A stage, where every man must play a part,
And mine a sad one.

GRATIANO

             Let me play the fool;
With mirth and laughter let old wrinkles come,   80
And let my liver rather heat with wine
Than my heart cool with mortifying groans.
Why should a man whose blood is warm within
Sit like his grandsire, cut in alabaster?
Sleep when he wakes? and creep into the jaundice   85
By being peevish? I tell thee what, Antonio,
(I love thee, and 't is my love that speaks):
There are a sort of men whose visages
Do cream and mantle like a standing pond,
And do a wilful stillness entertain,   90
With purpose to be dressed in an opinion
Of wisdom, gravity, profound conceit,
As who should say, "I am Sir Oracle,
And when I ope my lips, let no dog bark."

96   *therefore only* . . .. only because (they keep silent).

98–9   *If they should . . . fools:* If they did speak, those who heard them would be forced to call them fools and thus be damned ('Whosoever shall say to his brother thou fool, shall be in danger of hell fire', *Matthew* 5.22).

101–2   *But fish not . . . this opinion:* Do not use (the bait of) a serious expression to win (the fish of) a reputation (for wisdom).

104   *exhortation:* sermon, lecture. Puritan preachers often delivered long sermons, a practice which Gratiano's whole speech seems to be mocking.

108   *moe:* more.

110   *for this gear:* at this rate.

112   *neat's tongue:* ox tongue.
        not vendible: not saleable (i.e. an old maid – not marriageable).

113   *Is that anything now?:* What was all that about?

Questions

Lines 96–7. See Old Testament, *Proverbs* 17.28: 'Even a fool, when he holdeth his peace is counted wise: and he that shutteth his lips is esteemed a man of understanding.'

1 What does this comment of Gratiano's indicate is his opinion of Antonio's explanation of his 'marvellously changed' disposition?

2 Are we to take seriously Gratiano's suggestion that Antonio may be using his melancholy in order to create a reputation for wisdom?

3 Even Antonio cannot follow Gratiano's line of reasoning in this scene. How should the character be played, in your opinion?

O my Antonio, I do know of these   95
That therefore only are reputed wise
For saying nothing; when I am very sure,
If they should speak, would almost damn those ears
Which, hearing them, would call their brothers
    fools –
I'll tell thee more of this another time.   100
But fish not with this melancholy bait
For this fool gudgeon, this opinion.
Come, good Lorenzo, (*To the others*) – fare ye well a
    while,
I'll end my exhortation after dinner.

LORENZO
Well, we will leave you then till dinner-time.   105
I must be one of these same dumb wise men,
For Gratiano never lets me speak.

GRATIANO
Well, keep me company but two years moe,
Thou shalt not know the sound of thine own tongue.

ANTONIO
Fare you well; I'll grow a talker for this gear.   110

GRATIANO
Thanks i' faith, for silence is only commendable
In a neat's tongue dried, and a maid not vendible.

                              Exeunt GRATIANO *and* LORENZO

ANTONIO
Is that anything now?

BASSANIO
Gratiano speaks an infinite deal of nothing – more
than any man in all Venice; his reasons are as two 115
grains of wheat hid in two bushels of chaff: you shall

13

119   *What lady is the same:* who is the lady.
123   *disabled:* diminished.
124   *something:* to some extent.
      a more swelling port: a grander life-style.
125   *my faint means . . . continuance:* than my small means would let me
      maintain.
126–7 *Nor do I . . . noble rate:* And I am not complaining about having to
      lower my standing of living.
128   *fairly:* honourably.
129   *prodigal:* extravagant.
130   *gag'd:* pledged, bound by.
132   *from your love:* because of your love.
      warranty: right.
136–7 *And if it stand . . . honour:* If it is honourable, as you yourself always
      are.
138   *my extremest means:* all my fortune – my last penny.
139   *occasions:* needs, requirements.
140   *shaft:* arrow.
141   *fellow . . . flight:* an arrow similar in flight power, size and weight.
142   *with more advisèd watch:* observing more carefully.
143   *adventuring:* risking.
144   *I urge this childhood proof:* I use this example from childish experience.

Questions

1 What difference do you detect in Antonio's manner when he is
  alone with Bassanio?
2 What is the dramatic purpose of Bassanio's speech to Antonio in
  lines 122–34?
3 Antonio's response in lines 135–9 is something of an interruption.
  What does this suggest about his interest in Bassanio?

seek all day ere you find them, and when you have
them, they are not worth the search.

ANTONIO

Well, tell me now what lady is the same
To whom you swore a secret pilgrimage,   120
That you to-day promised to tell me of.

BASSANIO

'T is not unknown to you, Antonio,
How much I have disabled mine estate
By something showing a more swelling port
Than my faint means would grant continuance;   125
Nor do I now make moan to be abridged
From such a noble rate, but my chief care
Is to come fairly off from the great debts
Wherein my time, something too prodigal,
Hath left me gag'd. To you Antonio   130
I owe the most in money and in love,
And from your love I have a warranty
To unburden all my plots and purposes
How to get clear of all the debts I owe.

ANTONIO

I pray you, good Bassanio, let me know it,   135
And if it stand, as you yourself still do,
Within the eye of honour, be assured
My purse, my person, my extremest means
Lie all unlocked to your occasions.

BASSANIO

In my school-days, when I had lost one shaft,   140
I shot his fellow of the self-same flight
The self-same way, with more advised watch,
To find the other forth, and by adventuring both,
I oft found both; I urge this childhood proof

15

145 *pure innocence:* completely honourable and free from moral fault, like a child.
148 *self:* same.
150–1 *Or . . . or:* either . . . or.
150 *latter hazard:* second (risk) loan (which you will have given me).
152 *rest debtor:* remain in your debt.
153 *herein spend but time:* you are just wasting time on this matter.
154 *to wind . . . with circumstance:* to talk in such a roundabout way.
156 *making question of my uttermost:* in doubting that I would risk all I have on your behalf.
160 *I am prest unto it:* I am bound to do it.
161 *richly left:* left very well off (by inheriting a fortune).
163 *wondrous virtues:* great qualities of character.
165–6 *nothing undervalued to:* no less worthy than. The other Portia referred to is the wife of Brutus, one of the main characters of Shakespeare's *Julius Caesar,* famous for her courage and devotion to her husband.
170–2 *golden fleece . . . quest of her:* A Greek legend tells how Jason won the golden fleece from the King of Colchis (*Colchos*) and thereby regained his kingdom.

Questions

1 Lines 140–52. Explain the argument that Bassanio uses in requesting a further loan from Antonio.
2 Lines 153–60. Why is Antonio somewhat impatient with Bassanio?
3 Lines 161–74. What impression of Portia is Bassanio seeking to give here? How does this third speech of Bassanio's differ from the first two?

16

Because what follows is pure innocence.   145
I owe you much, and, like a wilful youth,
That which I owe is lost, but if you please
To shoot another arrow that self way
Which you did shoot the first, I do not doubt,
As I will watch the aim, or to find both,   150
Or bring your latter hazard back again,
And thankfully rest debtor for the first.

ANTONIO

You know me well, and herein spend but time
To wind about my love with circumstance,
And out of doubt you do me now more wrong   155
In making question of my uttermost
Than if you had made waste of all I have.
Then do but say to me what I should do
That in your knowledge may by me be done,
And I am prest unto it: therefore speak.   160

BASSANIO

In Belmont is a lady richly left,
And she is fair, and, fairer than that word,
Of wondrous virtues. Sometimes from her eyes
I did receive fair speechless messages.
Her name is Portia, nothing undervalued   165
To Cato's daughter, Brutus' Portia,
Nor is the wide world ignorant of her worth,
For the four winds blow in from every coast
Renownèd suitors, and her sunny locks
Hang on her temples like a golden fleece,   170
Which makes her seat of Belmont Colchos' strand,
And many Jasons come in quest of her.
O my Antonio, had I but the means
To hold a rival place with one of them,

17

175 *presages:* foretells.
    thrift: good fortune (from the verb 'to thrive').
176 *questionless:* doubtless.
178 *commodity:* goods to sell.
179 *a present sum:* ready cash.
180 *Try . . . can do:* See what you can borrow using my name as security.
181 *racked:* stretched.
182 *furnish:* equip.
183 *presently:* immediately.
184–5 *I no question make . . . or for my sake:* I shall not argue over whether it is a personal loan or a business arrangement.

Question

What does Antonio's reaction to Bassanio's request tell us about the relationship between the two characters?

---

1 *By my troth:* a mild oath – Honestly (troth = truth, faith).
5 *aught:* anything, all.
    surfeit: overeat.
7–8 *mean:* Nerissa puns on the two senses of the word 'mean': *no mean happiness* – no little happiness; *in the mean* – in average circumstances.
8 *superfluity:* over-indulgence.
    comes sooner by: acquires white hairs more quickly – makes one grow old quickly.
9 *competency:* moderation (makes one live longer).

18

I have a mind presages me such thrift 175
That I should questionless be fortunate.

ANTONIO

Thou know'st that all my fortunes are at sea,
Neither have I money, nor commodity
To raise a present sum; therefore go forth;
Try what my credit can in Venice do, 180
That shall be racked even to the uttermost
To furnish thee to Belmont to fair Portia.
Go, presently inquire, and so will I,
Where money is; and I no question make
To have it of my trust, or for my sake. 185

Exeunt

Scene two

Belmont. A room in Portia's house.

Enter PORTIA *with her waiting-woman* NERISSA.

PORTIA

By my troth, Nerissa, my little body is aweary of
this great world.

NERISSA

You would be, sweet madam, if your miseries were
in the same abundance as your good fortunes are;
and yet for aught I see, they are as sick that surfeit 5
with too much, as they that starve with nothing; it is
no mean happiness therefore to be seated in the
mean – superfluity comes sooner by white hairs, but
competency lives longer.

10 *sentences:* wise sayings.
13 *had been:* would have been. Portia says that if people could *be* good as easily as they *recognize* what is good, then there would be a need for more large churches rather than little chapels, and poor men could prosper like princes.
14 *divine:* preacher.
18 *blood:* emotions.
19 *decree:* rule.
19–20 The wildness of youth would ignore the advice of reason as a hare swiftly leaps over the nets set to capture it.
21 *not in the fashion:* not appropriate to.
24 *will:* Portia plays on the two meanings of the word.
30 *whereof who chooses:* by means of which the man who chooses.
31 *his meaning:* that is, Portia's father's hidden intention.
28–32 *the lottery . . . rightly love:* the person who chooses correctly (rightly) in the lottery will be the one whom you truly (rightly) love.
35 *over-name:* run through their names.

Questions

1 What does Portia mean by saying '*Is it not hard, Nerissa, that I cannot choose one, nor refuse none?*'?

2 What is Portia's mood here and what is its dramatic function, following as it does upon Bassanio's description of Portia in Scene 1?

3 In what ways can the social relationship between Portia and Nerissa be made clear to the audience at the beginning of the scene?

PORTIA

Good sentences, and well pronounced.   10

NERISSA

They would be better if well followed.

PORTIA

If to do were as easy as to know what were good to
do, chapels had been churches, and poor men's cot-
tages princes' palaces. It is a good divine that follows
his own instructions. I can easier teach twenty what   15
were good to be done than be one of the twenty to
follow mine own teaching; the brain may devise
laws for the blood, but a hot temper leaps o'er a cold
decree; – such a hare is madness the youth, to skip
o'er the meshes of good counsel the cripple. But this   20
reasoning is not in the fashion to choose me a husband. – O me, the word "choose"! I may neither
choose who I would, nor refuse who I dislike, so is
the will of a living daughter curbed by the will of a
dead father. Is it not hard, Nerissa, that I cannot   25
choose one, nor refuse none?

NERISSA

Your father was ever virtuous, and holy men at
their death have good inspirations; therefore the lottery that he hath devised in these three chests, of
gold, silver, and lead, whereof who chooses his   30
meaning chooses you, will no doubt never be chosen
by any rightly, but one who you shall rightly love.
But what warmth is there in your affection towards
any of these princely suitors that are already come?

PORTIA

I pray thee over-name them, and as thou namest   35

21

37   *level at:* aim at, estimate.

38   *Neapolitan:* of Naples, famous for horsemanship.

39   *colt:* young horse.

40   *appropriation:* addition.

41   *good parts:* accomplishments.

42   *afeared:* afraid.

42–3   *his mother . . . a smith:* his real father was probably a blacksmith.

44   *County Palatine:* ruler of a state (County = Count).

45   *as who should say:* as if he were saying.
      an: if.

46   *choose:* that is, choose whoever you like.

47   *the weeping philosopher:* A reference to Heraclitus, an ancient Greek philosopher who withdrew from the world because the folly of mankind depressed him.

48   *unmannerly:* inappropriate, unbecoming.

50   *death's head . . . mouth:* skull and crossbones, a 'memento mori' or reminder of death, often found on tombstones.

52   *How say you by:* What do you say about.

57   *throstle:* a thrush.

58   *falls straight a-capering:* starts dancing about immediately.

them, I will describe them. And according to my
description level at my affection.

NERISSA

First there is the Neapolitan prince.

PORTIA

Ay, that's a colt indeed, for he doth nothing but talk
of his horse, and he makes it a great appropriation 40
to his own good parts that he can shoe him himself.
I am much afeared my lady his mother played false
with a smith.

NERISSA

Then is there the County Palatine.

PORTIA

He doth nothing but frown, as who should say, "an 45
you will not have me, choose". He hears merry tales
and smiles not; I fear he will prove the weeping philosopher when he grows old, being so full of unmannerly sadness in his youth. I had rather be married
to a death's-head with a bone in his mouth, than to 50
either of these. God defend me from these two.

NERISSA

How say you by the French lord, Monsieur Le Bon?

PORTIA

God made him, and therefore let him pass for a
man. In truth I know it is a sin to be a mocker, but
he! why he hath a horse better than the Neapoli- 55
tan's, a better bad habit of frowning than the Count
Palatine; he is every man in no man; if a throstle
sing, he falls straight a-capering. He will fence with
his own shadow. If I should marry him, I should
marry twenty husbands. If he would despise me, I 60

62 *requite him:* return his love.

65 *I say nothing to him:* Portia deliberately misunderstands Nerissa's question which can mean either 'What do you think of . . . ?' (Nerissa's meaning) or 'What do you speak to him about . . .?'

67–8 *you will . . . swear:* you will testify.

68 *a poor pennyworth:* little or nothing.

70 *dumb-show:* mime. Some earlier Elizabethan plays began with a mimed outline of the plot.
    suited: dressed.

71 *doublet:* tunic.
    round hose: short breeches. The man who returned from abroad with items of clothing from several different countries was a common target of humour at the time.

75 *hath a neighbourly charity:* has friendly feelings, like a good neighbour. Portia is being ironical as England and Scotland were traditional enemies.

76 *borrowed a box of the ear:* received a blow on the ear.

77 *pay him again:* repay him.

78 *Frenchman . . . for another:* The Frenchman guaranteed this promise and undertook to add a blow of his own. France and Scotland were often allies against England – an arrangement called 'the Auld Alliance'.

84–85 *best* and *beast* were probably very similar in pronunciation in Shakespeare's day.

would forgive him, for if he love me to madness, I
shall never requite him.

NERISSA

What say you then to Falconbridge, the young
baron of England?

PORTIA

You know I say nothing to him, for he understands 65
not me, nor I him; he hath neither Latin, French,
nor Italian, and you will come into the court and
swear that I have a poor pennyworth in the English.
He is a proper man's picture, but alas! who can converse with a dumb-show? How oddly he is suited! I 70
think he bought his doublet in Italy, his round hose
in France, his bonnet in Germany, and his behaviour everywhere.

NERISSA

What think you of the Scottish lord, his neighbour?

PORTIA

That he hath a neighbourly charity in him, for he 75
borrowed a box of the ear of the Englishman, and
swore he would pay him again when he was able. I
think the Frenchman became his surety, and sealed
under for another.

NERISSA

How like you the young German, the Duke of Sax- 80
ony's nephew?

PORTIA

Very vilely in the morning when he is sober, and
mostly vilely in the afternoon when he is drunk;
when he is best, he is a little worse than a man, and

85–6 *An the worst ... fell;* if the worst comes to the worst.
86 *make shift:* manage.
92 *Rhenish wine:* German wine from the district of the River Rhine.
contrary casket: the incorrect casket.
95 *ere:* before.
sponge: drunkard.
99 *no more suit:* no further courtship.
100 *some other sort:* some different means.
100–1 *father's imposition:* conditions laid down by your father.
102 *Sibylla:* A prophetess who was granted her wish to live as many years as she had grains of sand in her hand.
103 *Diana:* the goddess of chastity.
104 *parcel:* pack.
106 *dote on:* long for.
109 *hither:* to this place.

Questions

Look back over Portia's description of each suitor.

1 What are the national characteristics of each suitor which Portia points out?

2 What characteristics of Portia herself do her descriptions of the suitors illustrate?

3 How does our impression of Portia at this point fit in with Bassanio's description in the preceding scene?

4 What is the dramatic function of this catalogue of rival suitors at this point in the play?

when he is worst he is little better than a beast. An 85
the worst fall that ever fell, I hope I shall make shift
to go without him.

NERISSA

If he should offer to choose, and choose the right
casket, you should refuse to perform your father's
will, if you should refuse to accept him. 90

PORTIA

Therefore, for fear of the worst, I pray thee set a
deep glass of Rhenish wine on the contrary casket,
for if the devil be within, and that temptation without, I know he will choose it. I will do anything,
Nerissa, ere I will be married to a sponge. 95

NERISSA

You need not fear, lady, the having any of these
lords; they have acquainted me with their deter-
minations, which it, indeed, to return to their home,
and to trouble you with no more suit, unless you
may be won by some other sort than your father's 100
imposition, depending on the caskets.

PORTIA

If I live to be as old as Sibylla, I will die as chaste as
Diana, unless I be obtained by the manner of my
father's will. I am glad this parcel of wooers are so
reasonable, for there is not one among them but I 105
dote on his very absence; and I pray God grant
them a fair departure.

NERISSA

Do you not remember, lady, in your father's time, a
Venetian, a scholar and a soldier, that came hither
in company of the Marquis of Montferrat? 110

123   *condition:* temperament.
125   *shrive me:* hear my confession (as a priest does).
126   *Sirrah:* You, fellow – a form of address used to servants.
       go before: lead the way.

Questions

1 Why are we told here that Portia already knows and admires Bassanio?
2 Why is she so cautious in speaking of him?
3 What is the dramatic effect of ending the scene with the announcement of the fifth suitor's arrival?
(Note how many scenes end like this one with a rhyming jingle.)

PORTIA

Yes, yes, it was Bassanio, as I think so was he called.

NERISSA

True, madam, he of all the men that ever my foolish
eyes looked upon was the best deserving a fair lady.

PORTIA

I remember him well, and I remember him worthy
of thy praise.   115

Enter a SERVING-MAN.

How now, what news?

SERVING-MAN

The four strangers seek for you, madam, to take
their leave; and there is a forerunner come from a
fifth, the Prince of Morocco, who brings word the
prince his master will be here to-night.   120

PORTIA

If I could bid the fifth welcome with so good heart
as I can bid the other four farewell, I should be glad
of his approach; if he have the condition of a saint
and the complexion of a devil, I had rather he
should shrive me than wive me.   125
Come, Nerissa. (*To the Serving-man*) Sirrah, go be-
    fore.
Whiles we shut the gate upon one wooer, another
    knocks at the door.

Exeunt

1 *ducat:* Italian coin, three of which were worth about one pound sterling.
4 *be bound:* be legally responsible.
6 *May you stead me?:* Can you help me?
11 *good:* wealthy or commercially sound (but Bassanio understands the word in relation to Antonio's character).
12 *imputation:* reference, accusation.

Questions

This scene, like the first in the play, begins in the middle of a conversation.

1 Why is this dramatically effective?
2 How should the entry of Shylock be staged so that the audience would recognize his importance as a character?

Scene three

Venice. A street.

Enter BASSANIO *with* SHYLOCK *the Jew.*

SHYLOCK

Three thousand ducats, well.

BASSANIO

Ay sir, for three months.

SHYLOCK

For three months, – well.

BASSANIO

For the which, as I told you, Antonio shall be bound.

SHYLOCK

Antonio shall become bound, – well.   5

BASSANIO

May you stead me? Will you pleasure me? Shall I
know your answer?

SHYLOCK

Three thousand ducats for three months, and Antonio bound.

BASSANIO

Your answer to that?   10

SHYLOCK

Antonio is a good man.

BASSANIO

Have you heard any imputation to the contrary?

15 *sufficient:* rich enough (to provide security for the sum required).
   in supposition: at risk (because not immediately available).
17 *the Rialto:* the Venetian Exchange where businessmen gathered.
19 *squandered:* wasted.
23 *notwithstanding:* in spite of all this.
25 *bond:* legal agreement.
26 *assured:* meaning both 'certain' and 'legally secure'.
28 *bethink:* consider carefully (how to safeguard my loan).
30 *pork:* As a strict Jew, Shylock would not eat pork.
   habitation: dwelling-place, location.
31 *Nazarite:* Jesus of Nazareth. See *Matthew* 8. 28–34 for the reference.

Questions

1 What is the significance of Shylock's description of Antonio's trading ventures?
2 Line 27. *assured:* What does Shylock's play upon the two meanings of the word suggest about his character?
3 What does Shylock's reference to pork and the Nazarite suggest about his knowledge of and attitude towards Christianity?
4 *Enter Antonio*: How should Antonio's entrance upon the stage be played here?

SHYLOCK

Ho no, no, no, no; my meaning in saying he is a
good man is to have you understand me that he is
sufficient. Yet his means are in supposition; he hath 15
an argosy bound to Tripolis, another to the Indies. I
understand, moreover, upon the Rialto, he hath a
third at Mexico, a fourth for England, and other
ventures he hath squandered abroad. But ships are
but boards, sailors but men; there be land-rats and 20
water-rats, water-thieves, and land-thieves, (I mean
pirates), and then there is the peril of waters, winds,
and rocks; the man is, notwithstanding, sufficient, –
three thousand ducats, – I think I may take his
bond. 25

BASSANIO

Be assured you may.

SHYLOCK

I *will* be assured I may: and, that I may be assured,
I will bethink me. May I speak with Antonio?

BASSANIO

If it please you to dine with us.

SHYLOCK

Yes, to smell pork, to eat of the habitation which 30
your prophet the Nazarite conjured the devil into. I
will buy with you, sell with you, talk with you, walk
with you, and so following, but I will not eat with
you, drink with you, nor pray with you. What news
on the Rialto? – Who is he comes here? 35

Enter ANTONIO.

BASSANIO

This is Signior Antonio.

37 *fawning:* flattering, wishing to curry favour.
   publican: Jewish tax-collector under the Roman empire. On the Elizabethan stage there was ample room for Shylock to speak these lines unheard by Antonio and Bassanio.
38 *for:* because.
39 *low simplicity:* humble foolishness, naïvety. Shylock may be speaking sarcastically of Antonio's straightforwardness in financial matters.
40 *gratis:* without charging interest.
41 *rate of usance:* interest rate.
42 *upon the hip:* a wrestling term meaning to catch an opponent at a disadvantage; a hold which preceded a throw.
44 *rails:* attacks verbally, strongly criticizes.
46 *well-won thrift:* hard earned profit.
49 *debating ... store:* working out what capital I have at the moment.
51 *gross:* total.
54 *furnish:* provide.
   but soft!: just a moment!
55 *rest you fair:* a greeting.
57 *albeit:* although.
58 *excess:* interest.
59 *ripe wants:* urgent needs.
60 *Is he yet possessed:* does he know already.

Questions
1 What are the reasons Shylock gives for his hatred of Antonio?
2 How do the phrases *our sacred nation* (line 44) and *cursed be my tribe* (line 47), referring to his Jewishness, contrast with Shylock's earlier reference to Christianity?
3 Compare *well-won thrift* (line 46) with Antonio's word *excess* (line 58). How do the connotations of these words point up the different attitudes of Shylock and Antonio towards financial dealings?
4 What is the dramatic function of Shylock's soliloquy here?

SHYLOCK (*Aside*)

How like a fawning publican he looks!
I hate him for he is a Christian:
But more, for that in low simplicity
He lends out money gratis, and brings down   40
The rate of usance here with us in Venice.
If I can catch him once upon the hip,
I will feed fat the ancient grudge I bear him.
He hates our sacred nation, and he rails,
Even there where merchants most do congregate,   45
On me, my bargains, and my well-won thrift,
Which he calls interest; cursed be my tribe
If I forgive him!

BASSANIO

Shylock, do you hear?

SHYLOCK

I am debating of my present store,
And by the near guess of my memory   50
I cannot instantly raise up the gross
Of full three thousand ducats: what of that?
Tubal, a wealthy Hebrew of my tribe,
Will furnish me; but soft! how many months
Do you desire? (*To* ANTONIO) Rest you fair, good
    signior;   55
Your worship was the last man in our mouths.

ANTONIO

Shylock, albeit I neither lend nor borrow
By taking nor by giving of excess,
Yet to supply the ripe wants of my friend,
I'll break a custom. (*To* BASSANIO) Is he yet possessed 60
How much ye would?

65 *Me thoughts:* I thought.
66 *upon advantage:* an interest.
67–70 *When Jacob . . . third:* Jacob was the third possessor of Abraham's property after his father Isaac. The story of how his mother helped him to disinherit his elder brother Esau is told in *Genesis* 27 and 30. Jacob was the founder of the nation of Israel. Shylock is implying his approval of such shady dealings.
74–84 *When Laban . . .:* This story is found in Genesis 30–39. The Elizabethan audience would have been familiar with the story.
74 *were compromised:* had come to an agreement.
75 *eanlings:* newborn lambs.
streaked and pied: striped and parti-coloured.
76 *hire:* payment.
rank: in heat.
78–9 *when the work . . . in the act:* when mating was taking place.
80 *pilled:* peeled the bark off (*me* has no separate meaning here).
81 *deed of kind:* sexual act.
82 *fulsome:* fertile.

Questions

1 Why does Shylock play for time by demanding a repetition of Bassanio's earlier information?
2 Why does Antonio interrupt Shylock's story?
3 From the entrance of Antonio, Shylock has begun to speak in blank verse rather than in prose. What does this change signify in dramatic terms?

SHYLOCK

Ay, ay, three thousand ducats.

ANTONIO

And for three months.

SHYLOCK

I had forgot – three months; (*To* BASSANIO) you told
    me so.
Well then, your bond; and let me see – but hear you,
Me thoughts you said you neither lend nor borrow   65
Upon advantage.

ANTONIO

I do never use it.

SHYLOCK

When Jacob grazed his uncle Laban's sheep –
This Jacob from our holy Abram was
(As his wise mother wrought in his behalf)
The third possessor; ay, he was the third ...   70

ANTONIO

And what of him? did *he* take interest?

SHYLOCK

No, not take interest, not as you would say
Directly interest; mark what Jacob did:
When Laban and himself were compromised
That all the eanlings which were streaked and pied   75
Should fall as Jacob's hire, the ewes being rank
In end of autumn turnèd to the rams,
And when the work of generation was
Between these woolly breeders in the act,
The skilful shepherd pilled me certain wands,   80
And in the doing of the deed of kind
He stuck them up before the fulsome ewes,

83 *eaning time:* lambing time.
84 *Fall:* gave birth to.
85–6 *This was a way . . . steal it not:* Shylock uses *thrive* as both 'prosper' and 'take legal profit'.
86 *served for:* was an agent for.
90 *Was this . . . good?:* Did you mention this to justify the charging of interest?
92 *breed:* It was an old idea that it was sinful to make money 'breed' money because metal is 'barren'.
94 *cite:* quote.
100 *the rate:* the rate of interest.
101 *be beholding:* be in debt.
103 *rated:* spoken harshly against.
104 *my moneys . . . usances:* financial dealings and interest charges.

Questions

1 *thrive* (line 85) and *thrift* (line 86): what was Shylock suggesting by using the same term to cover different activities within a biblical context?
2 Why should Shylock make such a lengthy defence of his usury?
3 Lines 87–91. What does Antonio's response to Shylock's biblical illustrations suggest about his character?
4 Lines 93–98. What clue to Antonio's melancholic attitude towards life does this speech offer?

Who, then conceiving, did in eaning time
Fall parti-coloured lambs, and those were Jacob's.
This was a way to thrive, and he was blest; 85
And thrift is blessing if men steal it not.

ANTONIO

This was a venture, sir, that Jacob served for,
A thing not in his power to bring to pass,
But swayed and fashioned by the hand of heaven.
Was this inserted to make interest good? 90
Or is your gold and silver ewes and rams?

SHYLOCK

I cannot tell, I make it breed as fast –
But note me, signior ...

ANTONIO

            Mark you this, Bassanio,
The devil can cite Scripture for his purpose;
An evil soul producing holy witness 95
Is like a villain with a smiling cheek,
A goodly apple rotten at the heart.
O what a goodly outside falsehood hath!

SHYLOCK

Three thousand ducats, 't is a good round sum.
Three months from twelve—then let me see the
    rate. 100

ANTONIO

Well, Shylock, shall we be beholding to you?

SHYLOCK

Signior Antonio, many a time and oft
In the Rialto you have rated me
About my moneys and my usances.
Still have I borne it with a patient shrug, 105

106 *sufferance:* ability to endure indignity and hardship patiently.
  badge: distinguishing feature. (In some European cities, Jews were obliged to distinguish themselves through wearing some special item of clothing such as a yellow cap.)

108 *gaberdine:* long cloak made of coarse material and worn by almsmen and beggars as well as Jews. (An interesting word, it may be connected with an older word for pilgrimage.)

111 *Go to, then:* And look at you now!

113 *void your rheum:* spit.

114 *foot:* kick.
  spurn: kick, also contemptuous rejection.

115 *suit:* request.

119 *bondman's key:* a slave's tone of voice.

120 *bated:* humbled through lowering his voice to a whisper.

126 *as like:* as likely.

129–30 *when did friendship . . . friend?:* when did a friend ever make money on a loan to a friend?

132 *break:* fail to pay when payment was due.

Questions

1 Lines 102–25. What different emotions are conveyed by Shylock in this speech? How does it differ from his earlier speeches?

2 Lines 126–33. What effect does Antonio's response have upon our assessment of his character thus far? How would he speak these lines?

For sufferance is the badge of all our tribe.
You call me misbeliever, cut-throat dog,
And spit upon my Jewish gaberdine,
And all for use of that which is mine own.
Well then, it now appears you need my help. 110
Go to, then, you come to me, and you say,
"Shylock, we would have moneys"; *you* say so;
You that did void your rheum upon my beard,
And foot me as you spurn a stanger cur
Over your threshold; moneys is your suit. 115
What should I say to you? Should I not say:
"Hath a dog money? Is it possible
A cur can lend three thousand ducats?"; or
Shall I bend low, and in a bondman's key,
With bated breath and whispering humbleness 120
Say this:
"Fair sir, you spat on me on Wednesday last;
You spurned me such a day; another time
You called me dog; and for these courtesies
I'll lend you thus much moneys"? 125

ANTONIO

I am as like to call thee so again,
To spit on thee again, to spurn thee too.
If thou wilt lend this money, lend it not
As to thy friends, for when did friendship take
A breed for barren metal of his friend? 130
But lend it rather to thine enemy,
Who if he break, thou may'st with better face
Exact the penalty.

SHYLOCK

                    Why, look you, how you storm!
I would be friends with you, and have your love,
Forget the shames that you have stained me with, 135

41

136   *doit:* a coin of very small value in Dutch currency – a scrap.
138   *kind:* meaning both 'generous' and 'according to my nature'.
140   *notary:* lawyer.
141   *single:* without conditions.
      in a merry sport: as a good-humoured jest.
145   *be nominated for:* be named as.
      equal: exact, equivalent.
148   *Content, in faith:* Done! An expression of agreement.
151   *dwell:* continue.
159   *break his day:* fail to pay up by the agreed date.

Questions

1 Lines 133–8. How do you account for Shylock's change of tune in this speech? What use does he make of Antonio's distinction between friends?

2 Lines 139 and 149. Explain exactly what Shylock's 'kindness' consists of.

3 What would be the most persuasive way for Shylock to speak these lines?

4 What causes Bassanio's change of attitude in lines 150–1?

5 What does Antonio's swift reassurance to Bassanio tell us about his character and temperament?

6 Lines 156–8. What light does Shylock's expostulation throw upon his nature? What does he hope to achieve by addressing this speech to Bassanio?

Supply your present wants, and take no doit
Of usance for my moneys, and you'll not hear me –
This is kind I offer.

BASSANIO

This were kindness.

SHYLOCK

                This kindness will I show.
Go with me to a notary; seal me there   140
Your single bond, and, in a merry sport,
If you repay me not on such a day,
I such a place, such sum or sums as are
Expressed in the condition, let the forfeit
Be nominated for an equal pound   145
Of your fair flesh, to be cut off and taken
In what part of your body pleaseth me.

ANTONIO

Content, in faith; I'll seal to such a bond,
And say there is much kindness in the Jew.

BASSANIO

You shall not seal to such a bond for me;   150
I'll rather dwell in my necessity.

ANTONIO

Why, fear not, man, I will not forfeit it –
Within these two months, that's a month before
This bond expires, I do expect return
Of thrice three times the value of this bond.   155

SHYLOCK

O father Abram, what these Christians are,
Whose own hard dealings teaches them suspect
The thoughts of others! Pray you, tell me this:
If he should break his day, what should I gain

43

160 *the exaction of the forfeiture:* insisting on the forfeit (the pound of flesh) being paid.
162 *profitable neither:* nor profitable.
165 *adieu:* farewell.
170 *purse . . . straight:* put the money into a bag at once.
171 *fearful:* insecure, untrustworthy.
172 *unthrifty:* careless. Shylock is much concerned with 'thrift' in money matters.
173 *Hie thee:* Away you go.

Questions

1 Lines 158–66. Comment on Shylock's meaning in these lines. Why should they convince Antonio yet elicit Bassanio's remark in line 175?

2 Why do Antonio and Bassanio take up such different attitudes to the signing of the bond?

3 Lines 173–4. Note Antonio's comment upon Shylock. Review this scene and outline the conflict between Antonio and Shylock which has existed until now. How far have their different religions contributed to this, in your opinion?

4 If producing the play, what variations in tempo would you suggest to reinforce the variation in emotional atmosphere?

5 If Antonio and Bassanio had been given soliloquies confiding their innermost thoughts and motives in this scene, what might they have said? Where would you have inserted them?

By the exaction of the forfeiture?   160
A pound of man's flesh taken from a man
Is not so estimable, profitable neither,
As flesh of muttons, beefs, or goats. I say,
To buy his favour I extend this friendship;
If he will take it, so; if not, adieu,   165
And for my love I pray you wrong me not.

ANTONIO

Yes, Shylock, I will seal unto this bond.

SHYLOCK

Then meet me forthwith at the notary's.
Give him direction for this merry bond,
And I will go and purse the ducats straight,   170
See to my house, left in the fearful guard
Of an unthrifty knave; and presently
I'll be with you.

Exit

ANTONIO

                    Hie thee, gentle Jew.
(*To* BASSANIO) The Hebrew will turn Christian, he
    grows kind.

BASSANIO

I like not fair terms and a villain's mind.   175

ANTONIO

Come on, in this there can be no dismay;
My ships come home a month before the day.

Exeunt

160   Stage directions. Notice the change of social context in this scene
      following on from the previous one.
      A flourish of cornets: a sound of horns announcing the entry of someone
      of high rank.
      a tawny Moor: olive-brown in complexion (note Shylock's phrase 'your
      fair flesh', in Act 1, Scene 3, line 144).
   1 *for:* because of.
   2 *shadowed livery:* dark (i.e. sunburned) 'costume'. The Prince compares
      the colour of his skin to a uniform worn by a member of a great house-
      hold – in his case, that of the sun god.
   5 *Phoebus:* the god of the Sun.
   6 *incision:* a cut which would draw blood was considered a symbol of
      courage.
   8 *aspect:* appearance.
   9 *feared:* frightened.
  10 *clime:* climate, country.
  12 *steal your thoughts:* win your heart.
  14 *nice:* well considered. Portia explains that her choice cannot depend
      on finding someone's appearance attractive.
  17 *scanted me:* restricted my choice.
  18 *hedged me by his wit:* in his wisdom limited me.
18–19 *to yield myself . . . I told you:* to give myself in marriage to whoever wins
      me in the manner I have told you about.
  20 *renownèd:* famous
      stood as fair: would have as good a chance.

Questions

1 What dramatic function does the sudden change in social context
  reflected in staging and language achieve in this scene?
2 What do we infer from Morocco's preoccupation with his appearance in his speech to Portia? What link, if any, can we make
  between this and the scene between Shylock and the Christians,
  Antonio and Bassanio?
3 Are we right to take Portia's answer as courtesy between social
  equals of high rank, or is she being ironic?

Act Two

Scene one

Belmont. A room in Portia's house.

A flourish of cornets. Enter the Prince of MOROCCO, *a tawny Moor, all in white, and three or four followers accordingly, with* PORTIA, NERISSA, *and their train.*

MOROCCO

    Mislike me not for my complexion,
    The shadowed livery of the burnished sun,
    To whom I am a neighbour, and near bred.
    Bring me the fairest creature northward born,
    Where Phœbus' fire scarce thaws the icicles,   5
    And let us make incision for your love,
    To prove whose blood is reddest, his or mine.
    I tell thee, lady, this aspect of mine
    Hath feared the valiant; by my love I swear,
    The best-regarded virgins of our clime   10
    Have loved it too. I would not change this hue,
    Except to steal your thoughts, my gentle queen.

PORTIA

    In terms of choice I am not solely led
    By nice direction of a maiden's eyes;
    Besides, the lottery of my destiny   15
    Bars me the right of voluntary choosing;
    But if my father had not scanted me,
    And hedged me by his wit to yield myself
    His wife, who wins me by that means I told you,
    Your self, renownèd prince, then stood as fair   20
    As any comer I have looked on yet
    For my affection.

24 *scimitar:* sword with a broad curved blade.
25 *Sophy:* ruler of Persia.
26 *three fields of:* three battles against.
    Sultan Solyman: Suleiman the Magnificent, famous ruler of Turkey.
27 *o'erstare:* outstare.
31 *alas the while:* 'alack the day', an expression of regret.
32 *Hercules and Lichas:* Hercules, the legendary Greek hero, famous for his great strength, sent his companion, Lichas, for a sacrificial garment which led to his death because it was poisoned. Morocco suggests that where the result depends on chance (*fortune*), strength and courage are irrelevant.
35 *Alcides:* another name for Hercules.
42 *be advised:* consider carefully.
43 *Nor will not:* Morocco promises not to propose to any other lady if he is unsuccessful.
44 *temple:* church. Morocco would presumably take an oath there.
45 *hazard:* gamble, chance, the taking of a risk.

Questions

1 What features of his character is the Prince of Morocco concerned to stress?
2 What is the dramatic function of this short scene?

MOROCCO

          Even for that I thank you;
Therefore I pray you lead me to the caskets
To try my fortune. By this scimitar
That slew the Sophy, and a Persian prince   25
That won three fields of Sultan Solyman,
I would o'erstare the sternest eyes that look,
Outbrave the heart most daring on the earth,
Pluck the young sucking cubs from the she-bear,
Yea, mock the lion when he roars for prey,   30
To win thee, lady. But alas the while!
If Hercules and Lichas play at dice,
Which is the better man, the greater throw
May turn by fortune from the weaker hand;
So is Alcides beaten by his page,   35
And so may I, blind Fortune leading me,
Miss that which one unworthier may attain,
And die with grieving.

PORTIA

              You must take your chance,
And either not attempt to choose at all,
Or swear before you choose, if you choose wrong,   40
Never to speak to lady afterward
In way of marriage; therefore be advised.

MOROCCO

Nor will not. Come, bring me unto my chance.

PORTIA

First, forward to the temple; after dinner
Your hazard shall be made.

MOROCCO

              Good fortune then,   45
To make me blest or cursed'st among men!

                   Sound of cornets. Exeunt

1	*serve me to run:* permit me to leave.
2	*the fiend:* the devil.
10	*Fia!:* Go away!
11	*for the heavens:* for Heaven's sake – an odd oath for a devil to use!
16–18	*did something smack . . . kind of taste:* had some faults. *Honest* means chaste as well as trustworthy.
23	*God bless the mark:* God forgive me! – an oath used in order to excuse an improper remark (such as mentioning the devil).
25	*saving your reverence:* another phrase of apology.
27	*incarnation:* Launcelot *should* say 'incarnate', i.e. in the flesh.

Question

What is the purpose of introducing Launcelot Gobbo at this point?

Scene two

Venice. A street.

Enter LAUNCELOT GOBBO, *the clown, alone.*

LAUNCELOT

Certainly, my conscience will serve me to run from
this Jew my master; the fiend is at mine elbow, and
tempts me, saying to me, "Gobbo, Launcelot Gobbo,
good Launcelot," or "good Gobbo", or "good
Launcelot Gobbo, use your legs, take the start, run   5
away." My conscience says, "No; take heed, honest
Launcelot, take heed, honest Gobbo," or, as
aforesaid, "honest Launcelot Gobbo; do not run,
scorn running with thy heels." Well, the most
courageous fiend bids me pack, "Fia!" says the   10
fiend, "away!" says the fiend, "for the heavens,
rouse up a brave mind," says the fiend, "and run."
Well, my conscience, hanging about the neck of my
heart, says very wisely to me: "My honest friend
Launcelot" – being an honest man's son, or rather   15
an honest woman's son, for indeed my father did
something smack, something grow to; he had a kind
of taste – well, my conscience says "Launcelot,
budge not!" "Budge!" says the fiend. "Budge not!"
says my conscience. "Conscience," say I, "you   20
counsel well; fiend," say I, "you counsel well"; to be
ruled by my conscience, I should stay with the Jew
my master, who (God bless the mark) is a kind of
devil; and to run away from the Jew I should be
ruled by the fiend, who (saving your reverence) is   25
the devil himself; certainly the Jew is the very devil
incarnation, and in my conscience, my conscience is

51

34 *true-begotten:* legitimately born. Another example of Launcelot's nonsense speech since the father begets the son, not vice versa. Launcelot gets his complicated words mixed up, probably because an Elizabethan of his class would have heard, not read, them – many in church services.

35 *sand-blind:* half-blind. 'Stone-blind' is completely blind so Launcelot's invention of 'gravel blind' suggests something in between.

36 *try confusions:* Launcelot means 'conclusions'. To try conclusions meant to test one's wits or strength against another.

40 *marry:* an exclamation derived from the name of the Virgin Mary meaning something like 'to be sure'.

41 *turn of no hand:* turn no way at all.

43 *God's sonties:* saints.

46 *'Master' Launcelot:* Launcelot gives himself a more dignified title which his father disclaims.

47 *raise the waters:* bring tears to the eyes.

but a kind of hard conscience, to offer to counsel
me to stay with the Jew; the fiend gives the more
friendly counsel: I will run, fiend; my heels are at 30
your commandment; I will run.

Enter old GOBBO *with a basket.*

GOBBO
Master young man, you I pray you, which is the
way to Master Jew's?

LAUNCELOT (*Aside*)
O heavens! this is my true-begotten father, who,
being more than sand-blind, high gravel-blind, 35
knows me not. I will try confusions with him.

GOBBO
Master young gentleman, I pray you, which is the
way to Master Jew's?

LAUNCELOT
Turn up on your right hand at the next turning, but
at the next turning of all on your left; marry, at the 40
very next turning turn of no hand, but turn down
indirectly to the Jew's house.

GOBBO
By God's sonties, 't will be a hard way to hit. Can
you tell me whether one Launcelot that dwells with
him, dwell with him or no? 45

LAUNCELOT
Talk you of young *Master* Launcelot? (*Aside*) Mark
me now, now will I raise the waters. (*To* GOBBO)
Talk you of young *Master* Launcelot?

GOBBO
No "master", sir, but a poor man's son. His father,

53

51 *well to live:* hale and hearty.

52 *what a will:* what he likes.

55 *ergo:* therefore (Latin). Launcelot is trying to impress with learned terms.

59 *father:* old man (though old Gobbo is, of course, Launcelot's real father as well).

60–1 *Sisters Three:* the three Fates of classical mythology who were responsible for human destiny.

61 *such branches of learning:* Launcelot is pretending a knowledge of classical learning.

64–5 *The very staff . . . prop:* my support in old age.

66 *hovel-post:* post round which a stack of corn was built.

68 *Alack the day!:* Alas!

though I say 't, is an honest, exceeding poor man, 50
and, God be thanked, well to live.

LAUNCELOT

Well, let his father be what a will, we talk of young
Master Launcelot.

GOBBO

Your worship's friend and Launcelot, sir.

LAUNCELOT

But I pray you, ergo old man, ergo I beseech you, 55
talk you of young Master Launcelot?

GOBBO

Of Launcelot, an't please your mastership.

LAUNCELOT

Ergo Master Launcelot. Talk not of Master Launcelot, father, for the young gentleman, according to
fates and destinies, and such odd sayings, the Sis- 60
ters Three, and such branches of learning, is indeed
deceased, or, as you would say in plain terms, gone
to heaven.

GOBBO

Marry, God forbid! The boy was the very staff of my
age, my very prop. 65

LAUNCELOT (*Aside*)

Do I look like a cudgel or a hovel-post, a staff, or a
prop? – Do you know me, father?

GOBBO

Alack the day! I know you not, young gentleman,
but I pray you tell me, is my boy, God rest his soul,
alive or dead? 70

74–5 *it is a wise . . . child:* Launcelot turns on its head the proverb: 'It is a
       wise child that knows its own father.'
  89   *thou:* Old Gobbo now begins to use the familiar form of 'you' to his son.
  92   *what a beard hast thou got!* Old Gobbo mistakes his son's hair for a beard.

Questions

Launcelot Gobbo is described as a 'clown'. This had two senses: first,
the part would be played by the clown or comedian of the company;
and second, Launcelot and his father are from the country, rustics.

Do you think that this scene was played for light relief in the action
or can you find any dramatic function for the relationship, the
dialogue, and the level of verbal humour involved?

LAUNCELOT

Do you not know me, father?

GOBBO

Alack, sir, I am sand-blind; I know you not.

LAUNCELOT

Nay indeed, if you had your eyes you might fail of
the knowing me; it is a wise father that knows his
own child. Well, old man, I will tell you news of 75
your son. (*Kneels with his back to* GOBBO) Give me
your blessing; truth will come to light, murder cannot be hid long – a man's son may, but in the end
truth will out.

GOBBO (*placing his hands on* LAUNCELOT's *head*)

Pray you, sir, stand up; I am sure you are not Laun- 80
celot my boy.

LAUNCELOT

Pray you, let's have no more fooling about it, but give
me your blessing; I am Launcelot your boy that
was, your son that is, your child that shall be.

GOBBO

I cannot think you are my son.   85

LAUNCELOT

I know not what I shall think of that; but I am
Launcelot, the Jew's man, and I am sure Margery
your wife is my mother.

GOBBO

Her name is Margery indeed; I'll be sworn, if thou
be Launcelot, thou art mine own flesh and blood. 90
(*He feels the back of* LAUNCELOT's *head*) Lord! (wor-
shipped might He be), what a beard hast thou got!

57·

94   *fill-horse:* cart-horse.
95   *grows backward:* i.e. shorter not longer.
100   *How 'gree you now?:* How do you get on with each other now?
101–2 *I have set up my rest:* I have made up my mind.
102–3 *run some ground:* covered some distance.
103   *a very Jew:* a Jew in every respect.
104   *a halter:* a noose (to hang himself with).
109   *rare:* very fine.
114   *hasted:* done quickly.
115–16 *put the liveries to making:* have the liveries (costumes befitting a grand household) made.
116   *anon:* at once.

Questions

1 What is the significance of Bassanio's entry at this point?
2 What connection can you see between Launcelot's description of his master to his father and Bassanio's instruction to his followers.

Thou hast got more hair on thy chin than Dobbin
my fill-horse has on his tail.

LAUNCELOT

It should seem, then, that Dobbin's tail grows back-   95
ward. I am sure he had more hair of his tail than
I have of my face, when I last saw him.

GOBBO

Lord, how art thou changed! How dost thou and
thy master agree? I have brought him a present;
how 'gree you now?   100.

LAUNCELOT

Well, well; but for mine own part, as I have set up
my rest to run away, so I will not rest till I have run
some ground; my master's a very Jew. Give him a
present? give him a halter! I am famished in his service. (*He makes* GOBBO *feel the fingers of his left hand,* 105
which he stretches out on his chest like ribs) You may tell
every finger I have with my ribs. Father, I am glad
you are come; give me your present to one Master
Bassanio, who indeed gives rare new liveries; if I
serve not him, I will run as far as God has any 110
ground. O rare fortune! here comes the man; to him
father, for I am a Jew if I serve the Jew any longer.

Enter BASSANIO *with* LEONARDO *and a follower or two.*

BASSANIO

(*To one of the men*) You may do so, but let it be so
hasted that supper be ready at the farthest by five of
the clock. See these letters delivered, put the liveries 115
to making, and desire Gratiano to come anon to my
lodging.

Exit the man

120 *Gramercy:* a shortened version of 'God have mercy', a common expression of surprise.
wouldst . . . me?: Have you any business with me?
124 *a great infection:* Old Gobbo means 'affection', desire.
129 *scarce cater-cousins:* hardly on speaking terms.
132 *frutify:* Launcelot means 'testify'.
135 *impertinent:* He means 'pertinent', relating to.

LAUNCELOT

  To him, father.

GOBBO

  (*To* BASSANIO) God bless your worship.

BASSANIO

  Gramercy, wouldst thou aught with me?   120

GOBBO

  Here's my son, sir, a poor boy –

LAUNCELOT

  Not a poor boy, sir, but the rich Jew's man that
  would, sir – as my father shall specify –

GOBBO

  He hath a great infection, sir, (as one would say) to
  serve –   125

LAUNCELOT

  Indeed, the short and the long is, I serve the Jew,
  and have a desire – as many father shall specify –

GOBBO

  His master and he (saving your worship's reverence) are scarce cater-cousins, –

LAUNCELOT

  To be brief, the very truth is that the Jew, having 130
  done me wrong, doth cause me, – as my father
  (being, I hope, an old man) shall frutify unto you –

GOBBO

  I have here a dish of doves that I would bestow
  upon your worship, and my suit is –

LAUNCELOT

  In very brief, the suit is impertinent to myself, as 135

139   *What would you?:* What do you want?

141   *defect:* meaning 'effect' or 'point'.

142   *obtained thy suit:* succeeded in your request.

144   *preferred:* recommended.
      preferment: promotion, advancement.

148–9 *A reference to the old proverb:* 'God's grace is gear enough' meaning 'God's grace is sufficient for one's needs'.

153   *more guarded:* more richly ornamented with bands of braid, woven cloth. It may, of course, refer to the ornamentation on a jester's coat.

154   *I cannot get a service:* I cannot get a place in service, in a gentleman's household.

156   *a fairer table:* a luckier palm. Launcelot is having fun with terms used in fortune-telling.

your worship shall know by this honest old man –
and though I say it, though old man, yet, poor man,
my father.

BASSANIO

One speak for both! – What would you?

LAUNCELOT

Serve you, sir.   140

GOBBO

That is the very defect of the matter, sir.

BASSANIO

I know thee well; thou hast obtained thy suit,
Shylock thy master spoke with me this day,
And hath preferred thee, if it *be* preferment
To leave a rich Jew's service, to become   145
The follower of so poor a gentleman.

LAUNCELOT

The old proverb is very well parted between my
master Shylock and you, sir; you have "the grace of
God", sir, and he hath "enough".

BASSANIO

Thou speak'st it well; (*To* GOBBO) go, father, with
thy son –   150
(*To* LAUNCELOT) Take leave of thy old master, and
inquire.
My lodging out. (*To his followers*) Give him a livery
More guarded than his fellows'; see it done.

LAUNCELOT

Father, in; – I cannot get a service, no! I have ne'er
a tongue in my head. (*He looks at the palm of his hand*) 155
Well, if any man in Italy have a fairer table which

157 *to swear upon a book:* take an oath (on the Bible).
158 *go to:* look here!
160 *aleven:* eleven.
coming-in: income (from dowry).
161 *scape:* escape.
161–3 *in peril . . . feather-bed:* Launcelot is contrasting escape from drowning with the danger of dying in bed – or simply falling out of bed.
164 *gear:* gift.
167 *orderly bestowed:* neatly stored.
168 *I do feast:* I am giving a banquet.
169 *best-esteemed acquaintance:* most highly regarded friend.
Hie thee: make haste.

Question
How does this scene affect our view of Bassanio?

doth offer to swear upon a book, I shall have good
fortune! Go to, here's a simple line of life, here's a
small trifle of wives; alas! fifteen wives is nothing,
aleven widows and nine maids is a simple coming-in 160
for one man, and then to scape drowning thrice, and
to be in peril of my life with the edge of a feather-
bed, here are simple scapes. Well, if Fortune be a
woman, she's a good wench for this gear. Father,
come; I'll take my leave of the Jew in the twinkling. 165

Exit with old GOBBO

BASSANIO
  I pray thee, good Leonardo, think on this;
  These things being bought and orderly bestowed,
  Return in haste, for I do feast to-night
  My best-esteemed acquaintance. Hie thee, go!

LEONARDO
  My best endeavours shall be done herein.   170

He begins to leave.

Enter GRATIANO.

GRATIANO
  Where's your master?

LEONARDO
  Yonder, sir, he walks.

Exit

GRATIANO
  Signior Bassanio!

BASSANIO
  Gratiano!

65

THE MERCHANT OF VENICE

175 *I have suit to you:* I have a favour to ask. (As on line 142 above, there is a play on the word *suit* meaning 'request' or 'favour' and *suit* meaning 'clothes' or 'livery'.)
178 *rude:* unmannerly.
179 *parts:* characteristics.
182 *too liberal:* free.
183–4 *To allay . . . spirit:* to restrain your high spirits.
185 *misconstered:* misconstrued, misjudged.
187 *a sober habit:* a serious and dignified manner.
190 *while grace is saying:* while grace is being said.
190–1 *hood . . . hat:* cover my eyes with my hat.
192 *observance of civility:* well-mannered behaviour.
193 *studied:* practised.
ostent: appearance.
195 *bearing:* behaviour.

Questions
1 Lines 177–86. How far does the tone of this speech reflect Bassanio's state of mind and his relationship with Gratiano?
2 Why is Gratiano so eager to go to Belmont and why is Bassanio willing to take him?
3 Lines 186–94. Compare Gratiano's speech with his earlier speech in Act 1, Scene 1, lines 79–102. How do you account for the difference in attitude between the two speeches?

66

GRATIANO

I have suit to you.

BASSANIO

You have obtained it.   175

GRATIANO

You must not deny me; I must go with you to
    Belmont.

BASSANIO

Why then you must – but hear thee, Gratiano;
Thou art too wild, too rude, and bold of voice,
Parts that become thee happily enough,
And in such eyes as ours appear not faults.   180
But where thou art not known, why, there they
    show
Something too liberal. Pray thee, take pain
To allay with some cold drops of modesty
Thy skipping spirit, lest through thy wild behaviour
I be misconstered in the place I go to,   185
And lose my hopes.

GRATIANO

Signior Bassanio, hear me:
If I do not put on a sober habit,
Talk with respect, and swear but now and then,
Wear prayer-books in my pocket, look demurely,
Nay more, while grace is saying, hood mine eyes   190
Thus with my hat, and sigh and say "amen",
Use all the observance of civility
Like one well studied in a sad ostent
To please his grandam, never trust me more.

BASSANIO

Well, we shall see your bearing.   195

67

196 *gauge:* judge.
199 *your boldest suit of mirth:* your most cheerful mood.
200 *That purpose merriment:* intend to have fun.

3 *Didst rob it ... tediousness:* took away some of the boredom.

GRATIANO

Nay, but I bar to-night; you shall not gauge me
By what we do to-night.

BASSANIO

No, that were pity;
I would entreat you rather to put on
Your boldest suit of mirth, for we have friends
That purpose merriment. But fare you well;   200
I have some business.

GRATIANO

And I must to Lorenzo and the rest;
But we will visit you at supper-time.

Exeunt

Scene three

Venice. A street.

Enter JESSICA *and* LAUNCELOT, *the clown.*

JESSICA

I am sorry thou wilt leave my father so;
Our house is hell, and thou, a merry devil,
Didst rob it of some taste of tediousness.
But fare thee well; (*She gives him some money*) there is a
    ducat for thee,
And Launcelot, soon at supper shalt thou see   5
Lorenzo, who is thy new master's guest;
Give him this letter, do it secretly;
And so farewell; I would not have my father
See me in talk with thee.

10   *exhibit:* malapropism for 'inhibit'.
11   *pagan:* non-Christian, a derogatory way of referring to her Jewishness.
11–12   *if a Christian . . . much deceived:* Launcelot seems to be referring both to the immediate future in which Lorenzo plans to abduct Jessica from her father, and to the possibility that since Jessica is generous and good-hearted she must have had a Christian rather than a Jew for a father. *Get* can mean both 'obtain' and 'beget'.
13   *something:* somewhat.
16   *heinous:* terrible.
19   *manners:* conduct and character.
20   *strife:* conflict (between duty as a daughter and love for a Christian).

Question

Do you find Jessica a sympathetic character on this, her first appearance?

---

1   *in:* during.
2   *Disguise us:* Wealthy young men enjoyed dressing up in masks for feasts and other celebrations.
5   *spoke us:* arranged, ordered.

LAUNCELOT

Adieu! tears exhibit my tongue, most beautiful 10
pagan, most sweet Jew! if a Christian do not play
the knave and get thee, I am much deceived; but
adieu! these foolish drops do something drown my
manly spirit; adieu!

Exit

JESSICA

Farewell, good Launcelot.   15
Alack, what heinous sin is it in me
To be ashamed to be my father's child!
But though I am a daughter to his blood
I am not to his manners. O Lorenzo,
If thou keep promise I shall end this strife,   20
Become a Christian, and thy loving wife!

Exit

Scene four

Venice. A street.

Enter GRATIANO, LORENZO, SALERIO *and* SOLANIO.

LORENZO

Nay, we will slink away in supper-time,
Disguise us at my lodging, and return
All in an hour.

GRATIANO

We have not made good preparation.

SALERIO

We have not spoke us yet of torch-bearers.   5

71

6 *vile:* it will fall flat.
   quaintly ordered: properly organized.
10–11 *An it . . . to signify:* If you open this (seal) it will tell you. Launcelot
   is again using words to give himself importance.
11 *hand:* handwriting.

SOLANIO

'T is vile unless it may be quaintly ordered,
And better in my mind not undertook.

LORENZO

'T is now but four of clock; we have two hours
To furnish us –

Enter LAUNCELOT, *with a letter.*

friend Launcelot, what's the news?

LAUNCELOT

An it shall please you to break up this, it shall seem   10
to signify.

LORENZO

I know the hand; in faith, 't is a fair hand,
And whiter than the paper it writ on
Is the fair hand that writ.

GRATIANO

Love-news, in faith.

LAUNCELOT

By your leave, sir.   15

LORENZO

Whither goest thou?

LAUNCELOT

Marry, sir, to bid my old master the Jew to sup to-
night with my new master the Christian.

LORENZO

Hold here, take this; (*He gives* LAUNCELOT *some
money*) tell gentle Jessica
I will not fail her; speak it privately, (*Exit*
LAUNCELOT)   20

73

22 *masque:* entertainment with music, dancing, and fancy dress or masks.
23 *provided of:* provided with. By *torch-bearer* Lorenzo means Jessica.
24 *Ay, marry:* Yes, indeed.
27 *some hour hence:* about an hour from now.
30 *I must needs:* I am compelled to.
32 *furnished:* provided.
33 *page:* a young boy attending his master.
36 *cross her foot:* cross her path.
37 *she:* i.e. misfortune (personified as female).
38 *she:* i.e. Jessica.
      issue to: offspring of.
      faithless: lacking true faith, an unbeliever.
39 *peruse:* study.

Questions

1 How do you account for Lorenzo's urgency in this scene?
2 How and why does Lorenzo try to show Jessica in a sympathetic light?

Go. – Gentlemen,
Will you prepare you for this masque to-night?
I am provided of a torch-bearer.

SALERIO
Ay, marry, I'll be gone about it straight.

SOLANIO
And so will I.   25

LORENZO
Meet me and Gratiano
At Gratiano's lodging some hour hence.

SALERIO
'T is good we do so.

Exeunt SALERIO *and* SOLANIO

GRATIANO
Was not that letter from fair Jessica?

LORENZO
I must needs tell thee all: she hath directed   30
How I shall take her from her father's house,
What gold and jewels she is furnished with,
What page's suit she hath in readiness.
If e'er the Jew her father come to heaven,
It will be for his gentle daughter's sake;   35
And never dare misfortune cross her foot,
Unless she do it under this excuse,
That she is issue to a faithless Jew;
Come, go with me, peruse this as thou goest.
Fair Jessica shall be my torch-bearer.   40

Exeunt

3 *gormandize:* overeat.
5 *rend apparel out:* tear (your) clothes through carelessness.
11 *bid forth:* invited out.
12 *wherefore:* why.
13 *love:* friendship.
15 *prodigal:* extravagant.
16 *right loath:* very unwilling.

Questions.

1 Lines 1–5. How does Shylock see himself as a master?
2 Why do you think Shylock has changed his mind about accepting Bassanio's earlier invitation to supper?

Scene five

Venice. In front of Shylock's House.

Enter SHYLOCK *the Jew and* LAUNCELOT *his man, who was the clown.*

SHYLOCK

Well, thou shalt see, thy eyes shall be thy judge,
The difference of old Shylock and Bassanio; –
(*He calls out*) What, Jessica! – (*To* LAUNCELOT) thou
     shalt not gormandize
As thou hast done with me – what, Jessica! –
And sleep, and snore, and rend apparel out. –   5
Why, Jessica I say!

LAUNCELOT

                    Why, Jessica!

SHYLOCK

Who bids thee call? I do not bid thee call.

LAUNCELOT

Your worship was wont to tell me I could do
nothing without bidding.

Enter JESSICA.

JESSICA

Call you? what is your will?   10

SHYLOCK

I am bid forth to supper, Jessica;
There are my keys – but wherefore should I go?
I am not bid for love; they flatter me;
But yet I'll go in hate, to feed upon
The prodigal Christian. Jessica, my girl,   15
Look to my house. – I am right loath to go;

17   *some ill . . . rest:* some harm coming which makes me ill at ease.

18   *to-night:* last night.

20   *reproach:* Launcelot means 'approach', though 'reproach' meaning 'unfavourable comment' would fit Shylock's attitude to Bassanio.

22   *conspired:* plotted. The irony in this choice of word becomes apparent shortly.

23–7 *it was not . . . the afternoon:* Launcelot delivers a nonsense speech parodying Shylock's earlier forebodings (see lines 17–18). He pretends to be able to interpret omens just as earlier he pretended to understand palmistry (Act 2, Scene 2).

30   *wry-necked fife:* a fife is a kind of flute played sideways giving the player a twisted neck.

31   *casements:* windows.

33   *varnished faces:* painted faces or perhaps masks.

35   *shallow fopp'ry:* empty nonsense.

36   *Jacob's staff:* When Jacob crossed the River Jordan he had nothing but his staff, though he went on to prosperity (*Genesis* 32.10). Notice how Shylock swears not by God but by the patriarchs of the Old Testament.

Question

What do we learn of Shylock's character from his speeches here, particularly in his attitude to masques?

There is some ill a-brewing towards my rest,
For I did dream of money-bags to-night.

LAUNCELOT
I beseech you, sir, go; my young master doth expect
your reproach.   20

SHYLOCK
So do I his.

LAUNCELOT
And they have conspired together; I will not say you
shall see a masque, but if you do, then it was not for
nothing that my nose fell a-bleeding on Black-
Monday last, at six o'clock i' th' morning, falling   25
out that year on Ash-Wednesday was four year in
th' afternoon.

SHYLOCK
What, are there masques? – Hear you me, Jessica,
Lock up my doors, and when you hear the drum,
And the vile squealing of the wry-necked fife,   30
Clamber not you up to the casements then,
Nor thrust your head into the public street
To gaze on Christian fools with varnished faces;
But stop my house's ears – I mean my casements,
Let not the sound of shallow fopp'ry enter   35
My sober house. By Jacob's staff I swear
I have no mind of feasting forth to-night;
But I will go. (*To* LAUNCELOT) Go you before me,
     sirrah;
Say I will come.

LAUNCELOT
                    I will go before, sir.

79

42 *worth a Jewess' eye:* There was a proverbial expression 'worth a Jew's eye' used for something of great value or profit. In medieval times, Jews had to pay fines on some occasions to escape having an eye put out.

43 *Hagar's offspring:* Hagar was an Egyptian servant of Abraham and her son, Ishmael, was an outcast and ancestor of Gentiles (*Genesis* 26).

45 *patch:* fool.

46 *snail-slow in profit:* very slow to do anything to benefit his master or to improve himself.

47 *drones hive not with me:* non-working bees will find no hive (home) with me.

50 *His borrowed purse:* the money he has borrowed.

53 *'Fast bind, fast find':* 'Whatever you make secure (fast) you will find safe (fast) when you return.' A proverbial expression.

55 *crost:* thwarted.

Questions

1 What do you learn of the father–daughter relationship in this scene?
2 What is the dramatic function of this scene in Shylock's household?

(*To* JESSICA) Mistress, look out at window, for all
    this –   40
There will come a Christian by
Will be worth a Jewess' eye.

Exit

SHYLOCK
What says that fool of Hagar's offspring? ha?

JESSICA
His words were, "Farewell, mistress"; nothing else.

SHYLOCK
The patch is kind enough, but a huge feeder,   45
Snail-slow in profit, and he sleeps by day
More than the wild-cat; drones hive not with me,
Therefore I part with him, and part with him
To one that I would have him help to waste
His borrowed purse. Well, Jessica, go in –   50
Perhaps I will return immediately –
Do as I bid you; shut doors after you –
"Fast bind, fast find" –
A proverb never stale in thrifty mind.

Exit

JESSICA
Farewell; – and if my fortune be not crost,   55
I have a father, you a daughter, lost

Exit

1   *penthouse:* overhanging roof. The roofed area at the back of the Elizabethan stage, with the upper stage above it, was probably used to represent Shylock's house in this scene.

2   *desired to make stand:* wanted us to wait.
      His hour is almost past: he is late.

4   *lovers . . . clock:* lovers are usually early rather than late.

5–7   *O ten times . . . faith unforfeited:* the doves (pigeons) which draw the chariot of the goddess of Love (Venus) fly ten times faster to confirm newly made vows of love than they would to maintain a relationship already established.

8   *That ever holds:* that's always true.

9   *that:* with which.

10   *untread:* retrace.

11   *tedious measures:* laboriously learned movements.
      unbated fire: unrestrained spirit and energy.

14   *younger:* a fine gallant, a young gentleman.
      prodigal: spendthrift, money-waster. (Shylock uses the same word about Antonio, Act 2, Scene 5, line 15).

15   *scarfed:* well-jointed with timbers strengthened. The word 'scarf' was beginning to get its meaning of a piece of clothing in Shakespeare's time thus *scarfèd bark* could also mean a ship decked out in flags.

16   *Hugged . . . wind:* embracing the ship with false welcome as a prostitute would embrace a rich, young gallant.

17   *she:* i.e. the ship. *The prodigal* refers to the biblical story in *Luke* 15. (Notice how the Christians' allusions are to the New Testament.)

18   *over-weathered ribs:* timbers weakened by bad weather.

19   *Lean:* referring back to *ribs.* The repetition of *strumpet* emphasizes the idea of the wind as a faithless woman.
      rent: torn.

Question

Lines 14–20. Why does Gratiano dwell in so much detail on this extended image?

Scene six

The same.

Enter GRATIANO *and* SALERIO, *dressed for the masque.*

GRATIANO
    This is the penthouse under which Lorenzo
    Desired us to make stand.

SALERIO
                          His hour is almost past.

GRATIANO
    And it is marvel he out-dwells his hour,
    For lovers ever run before the clock.

SALERIO
    O ten times faster Venus' pigeons fly   5
    To seal love's bonds new-made, than they are wont
    To keep obligèd faith unforfeited!

GRATIANO
    That ever holds; who riseth from a feast
    With that keen appetite that he sits down?
    Where is the horse that doth untread again   10
    His tedious measures with the unbated fire
    That he did pace them first? All things that are,
    Are with more spirit chasèd than enjoyed.
    How like a younger or a prodigal
    The scarfèd bark puts from her native bay,   15
    Hugged and embracèd by the strumpet wind!
    How like the prodigal doth she return
    With over-weathered ribs and ragged sails,
    Lean, rent, and beggared by the strumpet wind!

21 *for my long abode:* for my lateness.
25 *my father:* i.e. my (prospective) father-in-law.
27 *Albeit:* although.
35 *exchange:* changed appearance.

Questions
1 Why doesn't Jessica recognize Lorenzo immediately?
2 Why should the Elizabethan audience have found Jessica's 'exchange' and her embarrassment particularly amusing?

Enter LORENZO.

SALERIO
Here comes Lorenzo; more of this hereafter.   20

LORENZO
Sweet friends, your patience for my long abode;
Not I but my affairs have made you wait;
When you shall please to play the thieves for wives,
I'll watch as long for you then. Approach –
Here dwells my father Jew. Ho! who's within?   25

Enter JESSICA *above, in boy's clothes.*

JESSICA
Who are you? – tell me, for more certainty –
Albeit I'll swear that I do know your tongue.

LORENZO
Lorenzo and thy love.

JESSICA
Lorenzo, certain, and my love indeed;
For who love I so much? and now who knows   30
But you Lorenzo whether I am yours?

LORENZO
Heaven and thy thoughts are witness that thou art.

JESSICA (*Throwing down a box*)
Here, catch this casket; it is worth the pains.
I am glad 't is night – you do not look on me –
For I am much ashamed of my exchange;   35
But love is blind, and lovers cannot see
The pretty follies that themselves commit,
For if they could, Cupid himself would blush
To see me thus transformèd to a boy.

41   *hold . . . my shames:* light up my embarrassment.
42   *good sooth:* indeed.
      too light: too shameful – a pun on two meanings of the word 'light'.
43   *an office of discovery:* an act whereby something is revealed. Jessica refers
      to the holding of a torch or a candle.
44   *obscured:* kept in the darkness.
      So are you: i.e. so you are (obscured).
45   *garnish:* garments, disguised appearance.
47   *close . . . runaway:* the night which guards secrets (close) is rapidly fading.
48   *stayed for:* awaited.
49   *gild myself:* enrich myself. Jessica is jokingly referring to the painted
      (gilded) faces of the masters and perhaps to her own 'garnish' or
      decoration.
51   *by my hood:* Gratiano may be jokingly referring to and swearing by his
      master's hood and perhaps also alluding to the different kinds of hoods
      worn by members of different professions at the time.
      a gentle: a well brought up woman, with a pun on Gentile – non-Jew.
52   *Beshrew me:* Curse me – a mild oath.
57   *constant:* steadfast, loyal.

Questions

1 How would you describe the tone of the exchange between Jessica
   and Lorenzo in this scene?
2 Is there anything about Jessica which reminds us she is her father's
   daughter?
3 Do you think she deserves Gratiano's compliment?

LORENZO

Descend, for you must be my torch-bearer.　　　　40

JESSICA

What, must I hold a candle to my shames?
They in themselves, good sooth, are too too light.
Why, 't is an office of discovery, love,
And I should be obscured.

LORENZO

　　　　　　　　　So are you, sweet,
Even in the lovely garnish of a boy.　　　　45
But come at once,
For the close night doth play the runaway,
And we are stayed for at Bassanio's feast.

JESSICA

I will make fast the doors, and gild myself
With some more ducats, and be with you straight.　50

　　　　　　　　　　　　　　　　Exit

GRATIANO

Now, by my hood, a gentle and no Jew.

LORENZO

Beshrew me but I love her heartily;
For she is wise, if I can judge of her;
And fair she is, if that mine eyes be true;
And true she is, as she hath proved herself:　　55
And therefore like herself, wise, fair, and true,
Shall she be placèd in my constant soul.

Enter JESSICA, *below*.

(*To* JESSICA) What, art thou come? – On, gentlemen,
　away!
Our masquing mates by this time for us stay.

62 *Fie, fie:* an exclamation of impatience.
64 *the wind is come about:* the wind has veered and therefore the ship must sail at once to take advantage of it.
67 *on 't:* about it.

Questions

1 Is there anything significant about Antonio coming personally to reveal this news to them?
2 What contrast do you find between Bassanio's friends' manner of spending his last evening in Venice before setting off for Belmont and what we infer about Antonio's?

Flourish of cornets: The sound of horns in harmony add a ceremonial note to the forthcoming scene and also signifies the change of social context from the Venice street scene to the high-ranking household of Portia's Belmont.

1 *discover:* reveal.
2 *several:* different.

Exit with JESSICA *and* SALERIO; GRATIANO *is about to follow them.*

Enter ANTONIO.

ANTONIO
Who's there?   60

GRATIANO
Signior Antonio?

ANTONIO
Fie, fie, Gratiano! where are all the rest?
'T is nine o'clock; our friends all stay for you.
No masque to-night – the wind is come about;
Bassanio presently will go aboard;   65
I have sent twenty out to seek for you.

GRATIANO
I am glad on 't; I desire no more delight
Than to be under sail, and gone to-night.

Exeunt

Scene seven

Belmont. A room in Portia's house.

Flourish of cornets. Enter PORTIA *with* MOROCCO *and both their trains.*

PORTIA (*To her attendants*)
Go, draw aside the curtains and discover
The several caskets to this noble prince:-
(*To* MOROCCO) Now make your choice.

4   *who:* which.
8   *dull:* (1) lacking brightness (2) not sharp.
     blunt: (1) outspoken (2) not sharp.
9   *hazard:* risk. Notice the repetition of this word in Morocco's next speech.
12 *withal:* as well.
14 *back again:* once more.
19 *fair advantages:* worthwhile benefits.
20 *shows of dross:* worthless things.
21 *nor ... nor:* neither ... nor.
22 *virgin hue:* silver is likened to the colour of the moon, the goddess of chastity. Notice that Morocco's allusions are to the pagan gods of classical mythology, differentiating him from Christians and Jews and also marking his learning, his intellectual rank.
25 *even:* impartial.
26 *rated by the estimation:* (1) judged by your own estimate of yourself (2) judged by your reputation.
29 *to be afeared of my deserving:* to lack confidence in my merit.
30 *a weak disabling:* unworthy undervaluing.

MOROCCO

    This first of gold, who this inscription bears:

    "Who chooseth me shall gain what many men de-

       sire."   5

    The second silver, which this promise carries:

    "Who chooseth me shall get as much as he deserves."

    This third, dull lead, with warning all as blunt,

    "Who chooseth me must give and hazard all he

       hath."

    How shall I know if I do choose the right?   10

PORTIA

    The one of them contains my picture, prince;

    If you choose that, then I am yours withal.

MOROCCO

    Some god direct my judgement! let me see,

    I will survey th' inscriptions back again; –

    What says this leaden casket?   15

    "Who chooseth me must give and hazard all he hath."

    Must give – for what? for lead, hazard for lead!

    This casket threatens – men that hazard all

    Do it in hope of fair advantages;

    A golden mind stoops not to shows of dross,   20

    I'll then nor give nor hazard aught for lead.

    What says the silver with her virgin hue?

    "Who chooseth me shall get as much as he deserves."

    As much as he deserves! – Pause there, Morocco,

    And weigh thy value with an even hand; –   25

    If thou be'st rated by thy estimation,

    Thou dost deserve enough, and yet enough

    May not extend so far as to the lady;

    And yet to be afeard of my deserving

    Were but a weak disabling of myself.   30

    As much as I deserve! – why, that's the lady!

36 *graved:* engraved.
40 *shrine:* holy place, usually containing the relics of a saint. Saints are usually dead but Portia is thought of as a living (*mortal breathing*) one by Morocco in the intensity of his passion.
41 *Hyrcanian:* belonging to a wild region near the Caspian Sea.
   deserts: wild places (rather than barren sandy wastes).
42 *throughfares:* highways.
44 *watery kingdom:* ocean. Morocco is describing a storm when the sea seems to defy heaven and 'spit' in the face of the sky.
49 *Is 't like:* Is it likely.
   't were: it would be.
50 *base:* unworthy. Lead is a 'base' metal.
   it were: it (lead) would be.
51 *rib:* enclose.
   cerecloth: winding sheet. Dead bodies were usually wrapped in waxed cloth and enclosed in lead coffins.
52 *immured:* walled up.
53 *tried:* tested (assayed).
56 *A coin:* The Elizabethan gold coin called an angel had on one side the figure of the archangel Michael standing on the dragon.
57 *insculped:* engraved.
60 *thrive:* prosper.
61 *form:* likeness.

Questions
1 What is Morocco's valuation of himself?
2 How does Morocco's view of Portia affect our view of him?
3 Set out Morocco's reasoning in choosing the gold casket, in note form first and then in continuous writing.

I do in birth deserve her, and in fortunes,
In graces, and in qualities of breeding;
But more than these, in love I do deserve –
What if I strayed no further, but chose here?   35
Let's see once more this saying graved in gold:
"Who chooseth me shall gain what many men
    desire";
Why, that's the lady – all the world desires her.
From the four corners of the earth they come
To kiss this shrine, this mortal breathing saint.   40
The Hyrcanian deserts, and the vasty wilds
Of wide Arabia are as throughfares now
For princes to come view fair Portia.
The watery kingdom, whose ambitious head
Spets in the face of heaven, is no bar   45
To stop the foreign spirits, but they come
As o'er a brook to see fair Portia.
One of these three contains her heavenly picture.
Is 't like that lead contains her? – 't were damnation
To think so base a thought; it were too gross   50
To rib her cerecloth in the obscure grave; –
Or shall I think in silver she's immured,
Being ten times undervalued to tried gold?
O sinful thought! never so rich a gem
Was set in worse than gold. They have in England   55
A coin that bears the figure of an angel
Stamped in gold, but that's insculped upon;
But here an angel in a golden bed
Lies all within. – Deliver me the key;
Here do I choose, and thrive I as I may!   60

PORTIA

There, take it, prince, and if my form lie there,
Then I am yours!

93

63 *A carrion Death:* a skull picked clean.
65 *glisters:* glitters, glistens.
68 *But my . . . to behold:* to look only at the outward appearance (of gold).
72 *Your answer . . . inscrolled:* an answer like this would not have been set down for you.
73 *your suit is cold:* your courtship is over.
75 *heat:* passion, contrasted with the coldness (*frost*) of rejection and a life without love.
77 *tedious:* long drawn-out.
    part: depart.
79 *complexion:* character, perhaps with reference to his colour. 'Complexion' was first used to describe a person's temperament. The modern meaning derives from the association of temperament with skin colour. See also Act 2, Scene 1, line 1.

Questions

1 How would you describe Morocco's attitude to the loss of his hopes of gaining Portia as his bride?
2 How should this character be performed on stage, in your opinion?
3 What does Portia's final comment add to our knowledge of her character?

He unlocks the golden casket.

MOROCCO

                O hell! what have we here?
A carrion Death, within whose empty eye
There is a written scroll; – I'll read the writing.

> *All that glisters is not gold;*   65
> *Often have you heard that told.*
> *Many a man his life hath sold*
> *But my outside to behold –*
> *Gilded tombs do worms infold;*
> *Had you been as wise as bold,*   70
> *Young in limbs, in judgement old,*
> *Your answer had not been inscrolled –*
> *Fare you well; your suit is cold.*

    Cold indeed and labour lost;
      Then, farewell, heat, and welcome, frost!   75
Portia, adieu! I have too grieved a heart
To take a tedious leave; thus losers part.

                      Exit with his train

PORTIA

A gentle riddance. (*To her attendants*) Draw the cur-
    tains; go; –
Let all of his complexion choose me so.

                        Exeunt

1 *under sail:* setting off by ship.
4–5 *The villain . . . ship:* Shylock complained to the Duke of Venice (*with outcries raised the Duke*) when on his return he found his daughter and his money gone. As a result the Duke set off with him to search Bassanio's ship.
10 *certified:* testified to.
12 *passion:* emotional outburst.
13 *variable:* swinging from one mood and topic to another.
19 *double ducats:* a coin worth twice as much as a ducat.

Questions

1 How would you describe Solanio's attitude to Shylock's sense of outrage? How should the character be played, in your opinion?
2 Why does Salerio affirm that Lorenzo was not aboard Bassanio's ship?
3 What is the dramatic function of his scene? Why should the dialogue be presented in blank verse rather than in prose?

Scene eight

Venice. A street.

Enter SALERIO *and* SOLANIO.

SALERIO

Why, man, I saw Bassanio under sail;
With him is Gratiano gone along,
And in their ship I am sure Lorenzo is not.

SOLANIO

The villain Jew with outcries raised the Duke,
Who went with him to search Bassanio's ship.   5

SALERIO

He came too late; the ship was under sail;
But there the Duke was given to understand
That in a gondola were seen together
Lorenzo and his amorous Jessica.
Besides, Antonio certified the Duke   10
They were not with Bassanio in his ship.

SOLANIO

I never heard a passion so confused,
So strange, outrageous, and so variable,
As the dog Jew did utter in the streets:
"My daughter! O my ducats! O my daughter!   15
Fled with a Christian! O my Christian ducats!
Justice, the law, my ducats, and my daughter!
A sealèd bag, two sealèd bags of ducats,
Of double ducats, stolen from me by my daughter!
And jewels, two stones, two rich and precious
    stones,   20
Stolen by my daughter! Justice! find the girl!
She hath the stones upon her, and the ducats!"

25 *look he keep his day:* make sure he fulfils his bond at the appointed time.
27 *reasoned:* conversed.
28 *part:* divide.
29 *miscarried:* was wrecked.
30 *richly fraught:* with a valuable freight or cargo.
39 *Slubber not business:* Do not be careless or hasty in your affairs!
40 *stay . . . time:* wait until time has brought your affairs to a satisfactory condition.
41 *for:* as for.
42 *mind of love:* mind centred on thoughts of love (i.e. courtship).
44 *fair ostents:* impressive displays and demonstrations.
45 *conveniently become:* be appropriate for the occasion.
46 *even there:* at that very moment.

Questions

1 How has the mood of the two friends changed? How is this change reflected in the language of their speeches?
2 Why is so much direct speech included in Solanio's and Salerio's accounts of Shylock and Antonio in this scene?

SALERIO

Why all the boys in Venice follow him,
Crying, his stones, his daughter, and his ducats.

SOLANIO

Let good Antonio look he keep his day   25
Or he shall pay for this.

SALERIO

                Marry, well remembered, –
I reasoned with a Frenchman yesterday,
Who told me, in the narrow seas that part
The French and English, there miscarried
A vessel of our country, richly fraught;   30
I thought upon Antonio when he told me,
And wished in silence that it were not his.

SOLANIO

You were best to tell Antonio what you hear;
Yet do not suddenly, for it may grieve him.

SALERIO

A kinder gentleman treads not the earth;   35
I saw Bassanio and Antonio part;
Bassanio told him he would make some speed
Of his return. He answered, "Do not so;
Slubber not business for my sake, Bassanio,
But stay the very riping of the time,   40
And for the Jew's bond which he hath of me,
Let it not enter in your mind of love.
Be merry, and employ your chiefest thoughts
To courtship, and such fair ostents of love
As shall conveniently become you there."   45
And even there, his eye being big with tears,
Turning his face, he put his hand behind him,

48 *with affection wondrous sensible:* obviously moved with depth of feeling.
52 *quicken his embracèd heaviness:* enliven the melancholy that has seized him.

Questions

1 Compare and contrast the reactions of Shylock and Antonio to their losses.
2 How does Scene 8 affect our opinion of these two characters?
3 What are the dramatic functions of Solanio and Salerio in this scene?

   Servitor: servant
3 *election:* choice.
5 *wherein I am contained:* in which my picture is.
6 *nuptial rites be solemnized:* we shall be married with the Church's blessing.
8 *hence:* from here.
9 *enjoined by oath:* bound by my oath (obviously already taken).

Question

How is music used in Scene 9?

And with affection wondrous sensible
He wrung Bassanio's hand, and so they parted.

SOLANIO

I think he only loves the world for him.   50
I pray thee let us go and find him out
And quicken his embracèd heaviness
With some delight or other.

SALERIO

Do we so.

Exeunt

Scene nine

Belmont. A room in Portia's house.

Enter NERISSA *and a Servitor.*

NERISSA

Quick, quick, I pray thee, draw the curtain straight;
The Prince of Arragon hath ta'en his oath,
And comes to his election presently.

A flourish of cornets. Enter the Prince of ARRAGON, *his train, and*
PORTIA.

PORTIA

Behold, there stand the caskets, noble prince;
If you choose that wherein I am contained   5
Straight shall our nuptial rites be solemnized.
But if you fail, without more speech, my lord,
You must be gone from hence immediately.

ARRAGON

I am enjoined by oath to observe three things:–

101

10   *unfold:* reveal.
11–12   *if I fail of:* make a mistake about.
17   *injunctions:* conditions.
19   *so . . . me:* I have prepared myself in that way (i.e. by accepting the stated conditions).
     fortune: good luck.
22   *You . . . hazard:* You will have to look more beautiful before I risk choosing you (i.e. the lead casket).
25–6   *'many' . . . multitude:* By 'many' the ignorant mob may be meant.
26   *choose by show:* judge by appearances (but see Arragon's own earlier remark, line 22).
27   *fond:* foolish.
28   *martlet;* house martin.
30   *Even in . . . casualty:* in the very path of accident or misfortune, where there is least protection.
32   *jump:* agree.
33   *rank me with:* put myself on the same level as.
     barbarous: uncivilized.

Questions

1 Lines 17–18. Why do you think Portia gives Arragon these reassurances?
2 Explain why Arragon rejects the lead and the gold caskets. What light do these rejections throw upon his character?

First, never to unfold to anyone   10
Which casket 't was I chose; next, if I fail
Of the right casket, never in my life
To woo a maid in way of marriage;
Lastly,
If I do fail in fortune of my choice,   15
Immediately to leave you, and be gone.

PORTIA

To these injunctions every one doth swear
That comes to hazard for my worthless self.

ARRAGON

And so have I addressed me – fortune now
To my heart's hope! – Gold, silver, and base lead. 20
"Who chooseth me must give and hazard all he
    hath." –
You shall look fairer, ere I give or hazard.
What says the golden chest? ha! let me see,
"Who chooseth me shall gain what many men
    desire." –
What many men desire – that "many" may be
    meant   25
By the fool multitude that choose by show,
Not learning more than the fond eye doth teach,
Which pries not to th' interior, but, like the martlet,
Builds in the weather on the outward wall,
Even in the force and road of casualty.   30
I will not choose what many men desire,
Because I will not jump with common spirits,
And rank me with the barbarous multitudes.
Why, then, to thee, thou silver treasure house,
Tell me once more what title thou dost bear: 35
"Who chooseth me shall get as much as he
    deserves."

38 *cozen:* cheat, outwit.

39 *stamp of merit:* genuine nobility, as opposed to counterfeit or pretence. The image probably relates to real and forged coinage.

41 *estates, degrees and offices:* possessions, positions and important functions in society. *Estates* could mean both possessions and high rank.

42 *derived corruptly:* obtained by false or unfair means.
    clear: undisputed, fully deserved.

43 *purchased:* acquired or earned (rather than bought).
    wearer: the possessor.

44 *How many . . . stand bare?:* How many would keep their hats who now go bareheaded? In Elizabethan times, it was the custom for servants and inferiors to take their hats off in the presence of masters or members of the upper classes. Arragon suggests that if honour always went to those who actually deserved it, many who are now servants would be masters – a curious sentiment for a Duke!

46–7 *How much . . . of honour:* How many who deserve to be no more than low peasants would be separated from the truly honourable. The metaphor of gleaning suggested by *low peasantry* is carried on with the references to *seed* and *chaff*.

48 *ruin of the times:* (1) misfortunes (2) the corrupt state of the times.

49 *new-varnished:* appear in their true brightness. Arragon's speech on true and false nobility, while it is clearly related to one of the major themes of the play (outward appearance and inner truth), also touches on a topic much discussed at the time, namely the search for honour and titles by those anxious to establish themselves in the upper ranks of society.

51 *I will assume desert:* claim what is mine by right. (See Morocco's comments on *his* deserving to win Portia.)

54 *a blinking idiot:* probably a half-wit with a fool's cap, winking its eye. (A blinkard was a term for someone lacking mental perception.)

55 *schedule:* piece of writing.

Questions

1 Why does Arragon choose the silver casket?

2 How does his reasoning compare with that of the Prince of Morocco when confronted by the three caskets?

And well said, too; for who shall go about
To cozen Fortune, and be honourable
Without the stamp of merit? Let none presume
To wear an undeservèd dignity;   40
O that estates, degrees, and offices,
Were not derived corruptly, and that clear
    honour
Were purchased by the merit of the wearer!
How many then should cover that stand bare!
How many be commanded that command!   45
How much low peasantry would then be gleaned
From the true seed of honour! and how much
    honour
Picked from the chaff and ruin of the times,
To be new-varnished! – Well, but to my choice.
"Who chooseth me shall get as much as he
    deserves" –   50
I will assume desert; given me a key for this,
And instantly unlock my fortunes here.

He opens the silver casket.

PORTIA
Too long a pause for that which you find there.

ARRAGON
What's here? the portrait of a blinking idiot
Presenting me a schedule! I will read it.   55
How much unlike art thou to Portia!
How much unlike my hopes and my deservings!
"Who chooseth me shall have as much as he
    deserves"!
Did I deserve no more than a fool's head?
Is that my prize? are my deserts no better?   60

61   *distinct offices:* separate functions. Portia is saying that since Arragon is the offender (in choosing wrongly) he cannot be his own judge (as he tries to be in claiming that he has been unjustly treated).

63   *tried:* refined (the silver of the casket).

66   *shadows:* insubstantial appearances.

68   *I wis:* I know truly.

69   *Silvered o'er:* (1) outwardly fine in appearance (2) silver-haired (and therefore old enough to judge more wisely).

71   *I will . . . head:* I (the *blinking idiot*) will always be your guide. That is, you will always be a fool.

72   *you are sped:* your business is done.

73–4   *Still more . . . linger here:* the longer I delay, the more foolish I shall appear.

77   *Sweet:* sweet lady.

78   *wroth:* anger and grief.

80   *deliberate fools:* fools who make an outward show of intellectual argument.

81   *They have . . . to lose:* They have just enough wisdom to lose by using their intellect (*wit*). All their wisdom only leads them to make a wrong choice.

82   *heresy:* falsehood.

Questions

1 Compare Arragon's attitude before, during, and immediately after his choice with that of Morocco.

2 How do you account for their being willing, despite their own rank, to submit to Portia's father's conditions in order to win her?

3 Arragon is often presented on the stage as a figure of fun. Do you think this is justified?

4 Why are Morocco and Arragon chosen to precede Bassanio as suitors in this scene?

PORTIA

    To offend and judge are distinct offices,
    And of opposèd natures.

ARRAGON

                     What is here?
    (He reads from the scroll) The fire seven times
                tried this;
        Seven times tried that judgement is
        That did never choose amiss   65
        Some there be that shadows kiss;
        Such have but a shadow's bliss.
        There be fools alive, I wis,
        Silvered o'er, and so was this.
        Take what wife you will to bed,   70
        I will ever be your head.
        So be gone; you are sped.

    Still more fool I shall appear
    By the time I linger here;
    With one fool's head I came to woo,   75
    But I go away with two.
    Sweet, adieu! I'll keep my oath,
    Patiently to bear my wroth.

                    Exit ARRAGON *with his train*

PORTIA

    Thus hath the candle singed the moth;
    O these deliberate fools! when they do choose,   80
    They have the wisdom by their wit to lose.

NERISSA

    The ancient saying is no heresy,
    Hanging and wiving goes by destiny.

85   *what would my lord?:* what does my lord want? Portia, in a playful mood, snatches the messenger's mode of address to her (*my lady*) with *my lord*.

89   *sensible regreets:* genuine and substantial tokens of courtship.

90   *commends and courteous breath:* compliments and fine words of praise.

92   *likely:* promising.

94   *costly:* splendid, richly decked.

95   *fore-spurrer:* horseman who rides swiftly ahead.

97   *kin:* relation.

98   *high-day wit:* especially fine language, suitable for some festival celebration.

100   *post:* messenger.

      so mannerly: with such style.

101   *Bassanio . . . it be!:* if it be your (Cupid's or Love's) will, let it be Bassanio!

Questions

1 How do you account for Portia's high spirits?

2 What irony can you find in the messenger's description of Bassanio's style and gifts?

3 How do you account for Nerissa's exclamation at the news?

PORTIA

Come, draw the curtain, Nerissa.

Enter MESSENGER.

MESSENGER

Where is my lady?

PORTIA

Here; what would my lord?   85

MESSENGER

Madam, there is alighted at your gate
A young Venetian, one that comes before
To signify th' approaching of his lord,
From whom he bringeth sensible regreets,
To wit, besides commends and courteous breath,   90
Gifts of rich value. Yet I have not seen
So likely an ambassador of love.
A day in April never came so sweet
To show how costly summer was at hand,
As this fore-spurrer comes before his lord.   95

PORTIA

No more, I pray thee; I am half afeard
Thou wilt say anon he is some kin to thee,
Thou spend'st such high-day wit in praising him.
Come, come Nerissa for I long to see
Quick Cupid's post that comes so mannerly.   100

NERISSA

Bassanio, Lord Love, if thy will it be!

Exeunt

2 *yet . . . unchecked:* the report persists, without being denied.

3 *of rich lading:* with a valuable cargo.

3–5 *the narrow . . . flat:* the Goodwin Sands in the English Channel (*narrow seas*) is a dangerous stretch of water where many ships have been wrecked on the sandbanks just below the water.

6–7 *if my . . . her word:* If Rumour (*Report*, personified here as an old woman) is to be believed.

8 *in that:* i.e. with regard to the report of the wreck.

9 *knapped:* nibbled.

11 *slips of prolixity:* lapses into long drawn-out style.

11–12 *crossing . . . talk:* going against the rules of plain language.

15 *Come . . . stop:* Salerio impatiently asks Solanio to come to the point and make an end of his tale because the latter contradicts his own stated intention.

Questions

1 What have we learned to expect when Solanio and Salerio enter the stage?

2 How does Salerio's speech echo his earlier words in Act 1, Scene 1?

3 Why does Salerio use prose speech in this instance, having spoken in blank verse in the opening scene with Antonio?

Act Three

Scene one

Venice. A street.

Enter SOLANIO *and* SALERIO.

SOLANIO
Now what news on the Rialto?

SALERIO
Why, yet it lives there unchecked, that Antonio
hath a ship of rich lading wrecked on the narrow
seas – the Goodwins, I think they call the place, a
very dangerous flat, and fatal, where the carcases of   5
many a tall ship lie buried, as they say – if my gossip
Report be an honest woman of her word.

SOLANIO
I would she were as lying a gossip in that as ever
knapped ginger, or made her neighbours believe she
wept for the death of a third husband. But it is true,   10
without any slips of prolixity, or crossing the plain
highway of talk, that the good Antonio, the honest
Antonio – O that I had a title good enough to keep
his name company! –

SALERIO
Come, the full stop.   15

SOLANIO
Ha! what sayest thou? – why the end is, he hath lost
a ship.

111

19 *betimes:* in good time.
   cross: frustrate, thwart.

26 *the wings:* Picking up Shylock's word '*flight*', Salerio jokingly refers to Jessica's page-boy disguise as 'wings' and Solanio, in the next speech continues the metaphor of flight.

28 *fledged:* ready to fly.
   complexion: nature, tendency (cf Portia's remark about Morocco in Act 2, Scene 7, line 79).

29 *dam:* mother. Shylock puns on the word in his response.

31 *the devil:* referring not only to Satan but to Shylock himself who has just 'judged' Jessica. (Salerio is indirectly saying Jessica is blameless and only the wicked – such as Shylock or Satan – would condemn her).

32–3 *My own . . . years:* Shylock is indignant that his own child should rise against her father. Solario calling him '*old carrion*' (i.e. old, rotten flesh) deliberately misunderstands him as saying that his (Shylock's) physical desires (*flesh and blood*) are beyond his control.

34 *I say . . . my blood:* Shylock's repetition of *my* indicates his insistence on being taken literally. Jessica is his own child. The repetition suggests also that he sees Jessica as his possession, so much so that she is an actual part of himself.

Questions

1 Compare Shylock's refusal to accept wordplay applied to his own situation with his own grim humour in Act 1, Scene 2. What does this tell us about him?

2 Why do you think Solanio and Salerio feel they can bait Shylock with impunity?

SALERIO

I would it might prove the end of his losses.

SOLANIO

Let me say "amen" betimes, lest the devil cross my
prayer, for here he comes in the likeness of a Jew.   20

Enter SHYLOCK.

How now, Shylock! what news among the merchants?

SHYLOCK

You knew, none so well, none so well as you, of my
daughter's flight.

SALERIO

That's certain; I, for my part, knew the tailor that   25
made the wings she flew withal.

SOLANIO

Any Shylock, for his own part, knew the bird was
fledged, and then it is the complexion of them all to
leave the dam.

SHYLOCK

She is damned for it.   30

SALERIO

That's certain, if the devil may be her judge.

SHYLOCK

My own flesh and blood to rebel!

SOLANIO

Out upon it, old carrion! rebels it at these years?

SHYLOCK

I say my daughter is my flesh and my blood.

113

36 *jet:* a hard form of lignite which is a glossy black in colour. As a further contrast with white ivory, it is usually not valuable.
37 *Rhenish:* white wine from the Rhine district. Red wine was considered to be better for the blood than white wine.
40 *match:* bargain, also a reference to Jessica's bad 'match' with Lorenzo.
prodigal: Notice Shylock's use of the word which he has used earlier.
42 *was used to come:* was accustomed to coming.
smug: trim and self-satisfied.
43 *mart:* i.e. the Rialto.
Let him . . . his bond: let him take good care he keeps to his bargain.
45 *a Christian courtesy:* an act of Christian kindness – or grandness, in a social sense (i.e. not charging interest).
49 *to bait fish withal:* to use as bait to catch fish.
51 *hindered me half a million:* prevented me from making half a million (ducats) in profit.
55 *dimensions:* shape and size.
56 *affections:* wishes or desires where *passions* means emotions and feelings prompted by desires (*affections*).

Questions
1 Lines 40–6. What feelings does Shylock reveal in this speech, especially by his repetitions?
2 Lines 47–8. How has Salerio's mood changed and how do you account for it?
3 Why has Shylock reverted to prose in this scene?

SALERIO

There is more difference between thy flesh and hers 35
than between jet and ivory, more between your
bloods than there is between red wine and Rhenish.
But tell us, do you hear whether Antonio have had
any loss at sea or no?

SHYLOCK

There I have another bad match, a bankrupt, a prodi- 40
gal, who dare scarce show his head on the Rialto,
a beggar that was used to come so smug upon the
mart. Let him look to his bond! He was wont to call
me usurer; let him look to his bond! He was wont to
lend money for a Christian courtesy; let him look to 45
his bond!

SALERIO

Why, I am sure, if he forfeit, thou wilt not take his
flesh – what's *that* good for?

SHYLOCK

To bait fish withal; – if it will feed nothing else, it
will feed my revenge. He hath disgraced me, and 50
hindered me half a million – laughed at my losses,
mocked at my gains, scorned my nation, thwarted
my bargains, cooled my friends, heated mine enemies – and what's his reason? I am a Jew. Hath not
a Jew eyes? hath not a Jew hands, organs, dimen- 55
sions, senses, affections, passions? fed with the same
food, hurt with the same weapons, subject to the
same diseases, healed by the same means, warmed
and cooled by the same winter and summer as a
Christian is? If you prick us, do we not bleed? If you 60
tickle us, do we not laugh? if you poison us, do we
not die? – And if you wrong us, shall we not revenge?

64–5 *what is his humility?:* What sort of kindness (such as the humility advocated by Christ) is shown by the Christian?

66 *sufferance:* patient submission. (Recall Shylock's earlier use of this word in Act 1, Scene 2.)

68–9 *it shall . . . the instruction:* you may be sure that I will go one better than those who have taught me. Shylock is claiming that he has learned revenge – rather than humility – from the Christians.

79 *gone:* i.e. taken (by Jessica).

80 *Frankfort:* a German city (now Frankfurt) where a great fair was held twice a year.

80–1 *the curse . . . till now:* The Jews were considered by Christians to be accursed because of their treatment of Christ.

69 *our nation:* The Jews were named originally after Judah, a patriarch, and the tribe descended from him belonged therefore to his kingdom. Shylock refers to 'nation' and 'tribe' as though strongly conscious of his share in a collective identity. Viewed by the Christians as an alien, he nevertheless sees himself not merely as an individual or an outsider; he has a tribe, and a nation, as well as religious identity.

Questions

1 Trace the line of argument in Shylock's speech from his criticism of Antonio to his justification of revenge.

2 Is there any development in Shylock's feelings during this speech?

3 How do you think we are intended to respond to Shylock here? Why do Solanio and Salerio not answer his questions?

If we are like you in the rest, we will resemble you in
that. If a Jew wrong a Christian, what is his
humility? Revenge! If a Christian wrong a Jew, what   65
should his sufferance be by Christian example?
Why, revenge! The villainy you teach me I will
execute, and it shall go hard but I will better the
instruction.

Enter a SERVING-MAN *from* ANTONIO.

SERVING-MAN

Gentlemen, my master Antonio is at his house, and   70
desires to speak with you both.

SALERIO

We have been up and down to seek him.

Enter TUBAL.

SOLANIO

Here comes another of the tribe; a third cannot be
matched unless the devil himself turn Jew.

Exeunt SOLANIO *and* SALERIO *with the* SERVING-MAN

SHYLOCK

How now, Tubal! what news from Genoa? has thou   75
found my daughter?

TUBAL

I often came where I did hear of her, but cannot
find her.

SHYLOCK

Why there, there, there, there! A diamond gone cost
me two thousand ducats in Frankfort – the curse   80
never fell upon our nation till now, I never felt it till
now – two thousand ducats in that and other pre-

85   *hearsed:* coffined.

Question

Lines 79–92. What are the different feelings expressed by Shylock in this speech? How does his manner of speech reflect his emotional state?

cious, precious jewels. I would my daughter were
dead at my foot, and the jewels in her ear; would she
were hearsed at my foot, and the ducats in her 85
coffin. – No news of them? why, so! – and I know
not what's spent in the search: why thou – loss upon
loss! The thief gone with so much, and so much to
find the thief, and no satisfaction, no revenge, nor
no ill luck stirring but what lights on *my* shoulders, 90
no sighs but of *my* breathing, no tears but of *my*
shedding.

TUBAL

Yes, other men have ill luck too – Antonio, as I
heard in Genoa, –

SHYLOCK

What, what, what? ill luck, ill luck?   95

TUBAL

– hath an argosy cast away coming from Tripolis.

SHYLOCK

I thank God, I thank God! Is it true, is it true?

TUBAL

I spoke with some of the sailors that escaped the
wreck.

SHYLOCK

I thank thee, good Tubal; good news, good news: ha 100
ha! heard in Genoa!

TUBAL

Your daughter spent in Genoa, as I heard, one
night, fourscore ducats.

SHYLOCK

Thou stick'st a dagger in me – I shall never see my

105 *at a sitting:* at one time.
106 *divers:* many.
108 *but break:* except to go bankrupt.
114 *Out upon her!:* A curse upon her!
115 *turquoise:* A blueish stone often used in betrothal rings. It was supposed to change colour when any danger threatened and to reconcile any enmity between husband and wife.
    Leah: Shylock's wife.
119–20 *fee me . . . before:* hire me a (sheriff's) officer, book him a fortnight in advance. Sheriff's officers could arrest people for debt.
121–2 *for were he . . . I will:* if he (Antonio) were not in Venice, I would be free to carry on my business however I please.

Questions

1 How do Shylock's feelings change in this scene and how does his language convey them?
2 Does the fact that he is addressing a fellow Jew affect his mode of expression?
3 What impression do we receive of Tubal in this scene? How should this character be played, in your opinion?

gold again – fourscore ducats at a sitting, fourscore 105
ducats!

TUBAL

There came divers of Antonio's creditors in my
company to Venice, that swear he cannot choose
but break.

SHYLOCK

I am very glad of it – I'll plague him, I'll torture 110
him – I am glad of it.

TUBAL

One of them showed me a ring that he had of your
daughter for a monkey.

SHYLOCK

Out upon her! – Thou torturest me, Tubal – it was
my turquoise; I had it of Leah when I was a bach- 115
elor. I would not have given it for a wilderness of
monkeys.

TUBAL

But Antonio is certainly undone.

SHYLOCK

Nay, that's true, that's very true. – Go, Tubal, fee
me an officer, bespeak him a fortnight before – I will 120
have the heart of him if he forfeit, for were he out of
Venice I can make what merchandise I will. Go,
Tubal, and meet me at our synagogue – go, good
Tubal – at our synagogue, Tubal.

Exeunt

1   *tarry:* wait.
2   *hazard:* make your choice.
3   *forbear:* delay.
5   *would not:* do not wish to.
6   *Hate . . . quality:* hate would not give you this kind of advice.
7   *lest:* in case.
8   *And yet . . . thought:* the thoughts of a maiden should not be spoken aloud.
11   *I am forsworn:* I would be breaking my promise.
13–14 *But if you . . . forsworn:* if you do choose wrongly, you will make me sin by wishing I had broken my promise.
15   *o'er-looked me:* put a spell on me.
18   *naughty:* wicked. This word had a much stronger force in Shakespeare's day.
20   *though yours, not yours:* yours by right of love but not yet by marriage. *Prove it so:* If it turns out (that I am not to be your wife).
22   *peize:* piece out, draw out.
23   *eche:* eke out, extend.
24   *stay:* keep.
     election: (your) choice.

Questions

1 *It is not love* (line 4). Why do you think Portia says this?
2 What change do we see in Portia when we compare this speech with her earlier conversation with Nerissa in Act 1, Scene 2?
3 How does this speech convey the conflict within her at this point?

Scene two

Belmont. A room in Portia's house.

Enter BASSANIO, PORTIA, GRATIANO, NERISSA, *and all their trains.*

PORTIA

I pray you, tarry; pause a day or two
Before you hazard, for in choosing wrong
I lose your company; therefore forbear a while.
There's something tells me – but it is not love –
I would not lose you; and you know yourself,   5
Hate counsels not in such a quality.
But lest you should not understand me well –
And yet a maiden hath no tongue but thought –
I would detain you here some month or two
Before you venture for me. I could teach you   10
How to choose right, but then I am forsworn;
So will I never be; so may you miss me;
But if you do, you'll make me wish a sin,
That I had been forsworn. Beshrew your eyes;
They have o'erlooked me and divided me;   15
One half of me is yours, the other half yours –
Mine own I would say; but if mine, then yours,
And so all yours. O, these naughty times
Put bars between the owners and their rights!
And so though yours, not yours. Prove it so,   20
Let Fortune go to hell for it, not I.
I speak too long, but 't is to peize the time,
To eche it, and to draw it out in length,
To stay you from election.

25 *rack:* an instrument of torture often used to extract confessions from suspected traitors.

27 *What treason ... love:* Portia makes a play on the word *rack* which Bassanio uses to convey the intensity of his feeling, suggesting that treachery is mixed with his love if he feels like a traitor being punished to obtain a confession.

29 *fear:* doubt.

30 *amity:* friendship, harmony.

33 *enforcèd:* compelled.

36 *the very sum:* the whole total, all.

37–8 *when my ... deliverance:* when my torturer teaches me the words I must say to obtain my freedom.

44 *a swan-like end:* the swan is supposed to sing only when its death is near.

Questions

1 Why do you think Portia makes light of Bassanio's image of being tortured?

2 What does this exchange between the two suggest about their relationship? Compare this lovers' dialogue with the conversation between Lorenzo and Jessica in Act 2, Scene 6.

BASSANIO

> Let me choose,
> For as I am, I live upon the rack. 25

PORTIA

> Upon the rack, Bassanio? then confess
> What treason there is mingled with your love.

BASSANIO

> None but that ugly treason of mistrust,
> Which makes me fear th' enjoying of my love.
> There may as well be amity and life 30
> 'Tween snow and fire, as treason and my love.

PORTIA

> Ay, but I fear you speak upon the rack
> Where men enforcèd do speak anything.

BASSANIO

> Promise me life, and I'll confess the truth.

PORTIA

> Well then, confess and live.

BASSANIO

> "Confess and love" 35
> Had been the very sum of my confession.
> O happy torment, when my torturer
> Doth teach me answers for deliverance!
> But let me to my fortune and the caskets.

PORTIA

> Away then! I am locked in one of them; 40
> If you do love me, you will find me out.
> Nerissa and the rest, stand all aloof!
> Let music sound while he doth make his choice;
> Then if he lose he makes a swan-like end,

45–6 *That the comparison ... proper:* so that this comparison may be more appropriate.
46 *the stream:* on which the swan floats to its death. Portia means her tears.
49 *Even as the flourish:* just like the fanfare.
51 *dulcet:* sweet.
55 *Alcides:* another name for Hercules. He rescued Hesione, daughter of Laomedon, King of Troy, when she was chained to a rock as sacrifice to a sea-monster.
57 *stand for:* represent.
58 *the rest aloof:* the others standing apart.
 Dardanian: of Troy.
59 *blearèd visages:* faces smeared with weeping.
60 *the issue:* result.
61 *Live thou:* if you live.
62 *the fray:* the contest.
63 *Fancy:* romantic inclination, not founded on firm affection.
66 *engendered:* conceived.
70 *knell:* funeral bell.

Questions

1 Lines 40–62. How do the images Portia uses in her speech contribute to the general atmosphere of the scene at this point?
2 What does this soliloquy reveal to us about Portia's feelings?
3 Line 63. A song heightens the atmosphere of romantic suspense and has some bearing on the choice facing Bassanio. If he had been listening to it, would it have helped him to choose the right casket?

126

Fading in music. That the comparison   45
May stand more proper, my eye shall be the stream
And wat'ry death-bed for him. He may win,
And what is music then? Then music is
Even as the flourish, when true subjects bow
To a new-crownèd monarch; such it is,   50
As are those dulcet sounds in break of day
That creep into the dreaming bridegroom's ear,
And summon him to marriage. Now he goes,
With no less presence, but with much more love,
Than young Alcides, when he did redeem   55
The virgin tribute, paid by howling Troy
To the sea-monster. I stand for sacrifice;
The rest aloof are the Dardanian wives,
With blearèd visages come forth to view
The issue of th' exploit. Go, Hercules!   60
Live thou, I live; with much, much more dismay,
I view the fight, than thou that mak'st the fray.

A song to music whilst BASSANIO *comments on the caskets to himself.*

> *Tell me where is Fancy bred,*
> *Or in the heart, or in the head?*
> *How begot, how nourishèd?*   65

ALL
Reply, reply.

> *It is engendered in the eyes,*
> *With gazing fed, and Fancy dies*
> *In the cradle where it lies.*
> *Let us all ring Fancy's knell;*   70
> *I'll begin it, – Ding, dong, bell.*

ALL
Ding, dong, bell.

73–103   *So may the outward shows:* Bassanio muses on the idea that outward appearances are nearly always a bad guide to real worth.

74   *still . . . ornament:* continually deceived by outward finery.

75–7   *what plea . . . evil?:* what plea is there so wicked that it cannot be presented in a persuasive manner which hides its evil nature?

78–9   *What dannèd error . . . test:* what heresy (leading to damnation) is not justified by some serious scholar quoting a biblical text to support it?

81   *simple:* altogether evil.

85   *The beard . . . Mars:* Hercules, the Greek hero, and Mars the Roman god of War, are portrayed as having beards, a symbol (*to render them redoubted*, line 88) strength and courage.

86   *inward searched:* examined beneath appearances.

  livers white as milk: The liver was considered to be the seat of courage in the body and 'white livered' therefore signified being cowardly.

87   *excrement:* outward growth (i.e. the beard).

89   *purchased by the weight:* bought. The next four lines develop a criticism of artificial beauty achieved through cosmetics, false hair and other external aids. This was a popular topic of criticism of the time.

91   *lightest:* worthless, immoral (with a pun on light in weight).

92   *crispèd:* curled.

93   *wanton gambols:* flirtatious movements.

94   *supposèd fairness:* apparent beauty.

95   *dowry:* legacy.

96   *sepulchre:* grave (in which lies the original owner of the hair).

97   *guilèd:* deceiving.

99   *Indian:* The Elizabethans used the word 'Indian' to denote anyone of a dark complexion. The Elizabethan ideal of female beauty was that of blonde, blue-eyed paleness and the term 'Indian' signified the opposite of these qualities.

100–1   *The seeming truth . . . wisest:* in these deceitful times, there is so much outward show of truth that even the wisest people may find it difficult to tell the true from the false.

102   *Hard food for Midas:* Midas, the legendary king with the golden touch found that even the food he touched turned to gold.

103–4   *Nor none of thee . . . man and man:* Bassanio is speaking of the silver casket and of silver (money) as the common servant of all men.

104   *meagre:* plain, not showy.

Questions

1 What does Bassanio's speech add to our knowledge of his character? How far do you think he may be aware of being overheard?

2 What areas of life does he draw his examples of corruption from? Why should these illustrations lead him to conclude (*Therefore*, line 101) that the gold and silver caskets are not for him?

BASSANIO

So may the outward shows be least themselves;
The world is still deceived with ornament.
In law, what plea so tainted and corrupt,   75
But, being seasoned with a gracious voice,
Obscures the show of evil? In religion,
What damnèd error but some sober brow
Will bless it, and approve it with a text,
Hiding the grossness with fair ornament?   80
There is no vice so simple, but assumes
Some mark of virtue on his outward parts.
How many cowards whose hearts are all as false
As stairs of sand, wear yet upon their chins
The beards of Hercules and frowning Mars,   85
Who, inward searched, have livers white as milk?
And these assume but valour's excrement
To render them redoubted. Look on beauty,
And you shall see 't is purchased by the weight,
Which therein works a miracle in nature,   90
Making them lightest that wear most of it;
So are those crispèd, snaky golden locks
Which make such wanton gambols with the wind
Upon supposèd fairness, often known
To be the dowry of a second head,   95
The skull that bred them in the sepulchre.
Thus ornament is but the guilèd shore
To a most dangerous sea, the beauteous scarf
Veiling an Indian beauty – in a word,
The seeming truth which cunning times put on   100
To entrap the wisest. Therefore, thou gaudy gold,
Hard food for Midas, I will none of thee,
Nor none of thee, thou pale and common drudge
'Tween man and man. But thou, thou meagre lead,
Which rather threaten'st than dost promise aught, 105

108 *fleet to air:* vanish into thin air.
109 *As:* such as.
    rash-embraced: too hastily taken on.
111 *allay thy ecstasy:* restrain your expression of happiness.
112 *In measure . . . excess:* express our happiness in moderation; to restrain it from overflowing (with a pun on 'rein': hold back a horse).
114 *surfeit:* over-indulge, take too much of.
115 *counterfeit:* portrait.
    demi-god: one with almost god-like power of creation.
116 *come so near creation:* could have almost created (a living being).
    Move these eyes?: Do these eyes move?
117 *or whether:* or.
    the balls of mine: my own eyeballs. Bassanio wonders whether the eyes in the portrait really move or whether they only seem to do so because of the motion of his own eyes as he scans the face.
118 *severed:* separated.
123 *faster:* more securely.
126 *unfurnished:* unaccompanied. The radiance of Portia's eyes is so great that when the artist had finished painting one of them, it would have so dazzled him that he would have been unable to complete the other.
127–9 *The substance . . . the substance:* Bassanio uses *substance* first to mean 'the whole' (of his praise) and then to mean 'the reality', i.e. Portia herself. Thus his inability to do justice by his words to the portrait is matched by the inability of the portrait, fine as it is, to do justice to the living woman.
130 *continent:* container.

Questions

1 Lines 120–3. Do you find Bassanio's image for Portia's hair appropriate?
2 How would you describe his reaction to having chosen the right casket?

Thy paleness moves me more than eloquence,
And here choose I; joy be the consequence!

PORTIA (*Aside*)

How all the other passions fleet to air,
As doubtful thoughts, and rash-embraced despair,
And shudd'ring fear, and green-eyed jealousy.   110
O love, be moderate, allay thy ecstasy!
In measure rain thy join, scant this excess!
I feel too much thy blessing; make it less
For fear I surfeit!

BASSANIO

What find I here?

He opens the lead casket.

Fair Portia's counterfeit! What demi-god   115
Hath come so near creation? Move these eyes?
Or whether (riding on the balls of mine)
Seem they in motion? Here are severed lips
Parted with sugar breath; so sweet a bar
Should sunder such sweet friends. Here in her hairs 120
The painter plays the spider, and hath woven
A golden mesh t' entrap the hearts of men
Faster than gnats in cobwebs. But her eyes!
How could he see to do them? having made one,
Methinks it should have power to steal both his   125
And leave itself unfurnished. Yet look how far
The substance of my praise doth wrong this shadow
In underprizing it, so far this shadow
Doth limp behind the substance. Here's the scroll,
The continent and summary of my fortune.   130

You that choose not by the view,
Chance as fair, and choose as true!

131

136 *hold your . . . bliss:* consider your good fortune to be your happiness.

140 *by note:* Bassanio jokingly puns on 'note' meaning (1) the words on the scroll, and (2) a bill of goods used in commerce.

141 *prize:* contest.

148 *confirmed , signed, ratified:* terms used in law and commerce, following on from Bassanio's use of *note* in line 140 above.

156 *livings:* properties. Many Elizabethan noblemen had the right to grant 'livings' or clerical appointments.

157 *Exceed account:* surpass estimation. The word echoes *account* in line 155.

158 *sum of – something:* Portia may be hesitating here in case it sounded as if she was boasting of her wealth and qualities, and deliberately ends on a modest note.

to term in gross: to give as a total amount.

159 *unpractised:* inexperienced.

163 *gentle:* meek, teachable.

Questions

1 Lines 141–8. How does Bassanio respond in this speech to his winning of Portia?

2 How far does Portia's response to Bassanio's success contrast spiritual and material aspects of love?

3 When Portia refers to herself as an *unlessoned girl* (line 159) and to *her gentle spirit*, how does this accord with the view you have formed of her character so far?

Since this fortune falls to you,
Be content, and seek no new.
If you be well pleased with this,   135
And hold your fortune for your bliss,
Turn you where your lady is,
And claim her with a loving kiss.

A gentle scroll. Fair lady, by your leave,
I come by note to give, and to receive.   140
(*He kisses her*) Like one of two contending in a prize
That thinks he hath done well in people's eyes,
Hearing applause and universal shout,
Giddy in spirit, still gazing in a doubt
Whether those peals of praise be his or no,   145
So, thrice-fair lady, stand I even so,
As doubtful whether what I see be true,
Until confirmed, signed, ratified by you.

PORTIA
You see me, Lord Bassanio, where I stand,
Such as I am; though for myself alone   150
I would not be ambitious in my wish
To wish myself much better, yet for you,
I would be trebled twenty times myself,
A thousand times more fair, ten thousand times
    more rich,
That only to stand high in your account,   155
I might in virtues, beauties, livings, friends
Exceed account. But the full sum of me
Is sum of – something: which, to term in gross,
Is an unlessoned girl, unschooled, unpractised;
Happy in this, she is not yet so old   160
But she may learn; happier than this,
She is not bred so dull but she can learn;
Happiest of all, is that her gentle spirit

167 *converted:* transferred – another commercial term.
    But now: just now, up to this moment.
169 *but now:* at this moment, even as I speak.
173 *presage:* foretell, forebode.
174 *vantage:* my right.
175 *bereft:* robbed, deprived.
177 *powers:* faculties.
178 *fairly spoke:* well spoken.
181–2 *Where every something . . . of joy:* all the different sounds of the crowd
    mingle together making one sound expressing nothing but the
    crowd's happiness.

Questions

1 Compare this speech of Portia's (lines 149–74) with that in which
  Bassanio originally speaks of his intended courtship of her to
  Antonio in Act 1, Scene 1.
2 What does the speech add to our knowledge of her?
3 What does the giving of the ring signify to Portia?
4 Lines 175–85. Bassanio's words accept and confirm Portia's sense
  of the ring's importance. What does the image *some oration* etc. line 178)
  indicate about his estimate of the relationship between Portia and
  himself?
5 Look back at Bassanio's speeches after the opening of the casket
  to this point (line 185). Trace the course of his feelings as he
  realizes that he has won her. Look particularly at *Fair lady, by your
  leave* (line 139) and *Madam, you have bereft me of all words* (line 175).

Commits itself to yours to be directed,
As from her lord, her governor, her king.   165
Myself, and what is mine, to you and yours
Is now converted. But now I was the lord
Of this fair mansion, master of my servants,
Queen o'er myself; and even now, but now,
This house, these servants, and this same myself   170
Are yours, my lord! I give them with this ring,
Which when you part from, lose, or give away,
Let it presage the ruin of your love,
And be my vantage to exclaim on you.

BASSANIO

Madam, you have bereft me of all words;   175
Only my blood speaks to you in my veins,
And there is such confusion in my powers,
As after some oration fairly spoke
By a belovèd prince, there doth appear
Among the buzzing pleasèd multitude –   180
Where every something being blent together,
Turns to a wild of nothing, save of joy
Expressed, and not expressed. But when this ring
Parts from this finger, then parts life from hence; –
O, then be bold to say Bassanio's dead!   185

NERISSA

My lord and lady, it is now our time
That have stood by and seen our wishes prosper,
To cry "good joy". Good joy, my lord and lady!

GRATIANO

My lord Bassanio, and my gentle lady,
I wish you all the joy that *you* can wish;   190
For I am sure you can wish none from me.

135

192	*your honours:* a respectful form of 'you'.
	solemnize: go through the marriage ceremony in church.
195	*so:* so long as.
197	*swift:* quickly.
199–200	*for intermission ... than you:* I do not delay any longer than you.
202	*as the matter falls:* as things have turned out.
204	*roof:* i.e. of his mouth.
206	*of:* from.
207	*fortune:* good luck – perhaps an irony is intended here since Bassanio had no 'fortune' in a material sense.

And when your honours mean to solemnize
The bargain of your faith, I do beseech you
Even at that time I may be married too.

BASSANIO

With all my heart, so thou canst get a wife.   195

GRATIANO

I thank your lordship, you have got me one.
My eyes, my lord, can look as swift as yours:
You saw the mistress, I beheld the maid;
You loved, I loved; – for intermission
No more pertains to me, my lord, than you.   200
Your fortune stood upon the caskets there,
And so did mine too, as the matter falls;
For wooing here until I sweat again,
And swearing till my very roof was dry
With oaths of love, at last, if promise last,   205
I got a promise of this fair one here
To have her love, provided that your fortune
Achieved her mistress.

PORTIA

                    Is this true, Nerissa?

NERISSA

Madam, it is, so you stand pleased withal.

BASSANIO

And do you, Gratiano, mean good faith?   210

GRATIANO

Yes, faith, my lord.

BASSANIO

Our feast shall be much honoured in your marriage.

137

213   *play:* make a bet (that whoever gets a son first will win a thousand ducats).

215   *stake down:* put down stake money. Gratiano follows this with an obscene pun on *stake.*

217   *infidel:* heathen, non-Christian, i.e. Jessica.

220   *youth of my new int'rest here:* the newness (youth) of my authority (interest) in this place – compare with Shylock's use of the word.

222   *very:* true.

231   *commends him:* sends his greeting.

Questions

1 What effect does Gratiano's news for Bassanio about his relationship with Nerissa have upon the emotional atmosphere of the scene at this point?

2 What does the entrance of Salerio signify?

GRATIANO

    We'll play with them the first boy for a thousand
    ducats.

NERISSA

    What! and stake down?   215

GRATIANO

    No, we shall ne'er win at that sport and stake down.
    But who comes here? Lorenzo and his infidel!
    What! and my old Venetian friend Salerio?

Enter LORENZO, JESSICA, *and* SALERIO.

BASSANIO

    Lorenzo and Salerio, welcome hither,
    If that the youth of my new int'rest here   220
    Have power to bid you welcome. By your leave
    I bid my very friends and countrymen,
    Sweet Portia, welcome.

PORTIA

                So do I my lord;
    They are entirely welcome.

LORENZO

    I thank your honour. – For my part, my lord,   225
    My purpose was not to have seen you here,
    But meeting with Salerio by the way,
    He did entreat me, past all saying nay,
    To come with him along.

SALERIO

                I did, my lord,
    And I have reason for it. Signior Antonio   230
    Commends him to you.

He gives BASSANIO *a letter.*

231 *Ere I ope:* before I open.
234 *well:* (1) in good spirits (2) financially well off.
236 *cheer yon stranger:* greet that stranger over there.
238 *royal:* princely in character and wealth (not literally a king).
240 *We are the Jasons:* cf Act 1, Scene 1, line 172.
241 *fleece:* a punning reference to Antonio's fleets.
242 *shrewd contents:* bad news.
245–6 *Could turn . . . constant man:* could so alter the appearance of any normal man.
247 *with leave:* with respect, 'please'.

Questions

1 What does Gratiano's exulting boast to Salerio (line 240) indicate about his character?

2 Why do you think Salerio speaks so drily and briefly to Bassanio and Gratiano at this point?

BASSANIO

                Ere I ope his letter,
I pray you tell me how my good friend doth.

SALERIO

Not sick, my lord, unless it be in mind,
Nor well, unless in mind; his letter there
Will show you his estate.   235

BASSANIO *opens the letter*.

GRATIANO

Nerissa, cheer yon stranger, bid her welcome.
Your hand, Salerio (*They shake hands*) what's the news
  from Venice?
How doth that royal merchant, good Antonio?
I know he will be glad of our success;
We are the Jasons, we have won the fleece.   240

SALERIO

I would you had won the fleece that he hath lost.

PORTIA

There are some shrewd contents in yon same paper,
That steals the colour from Bassanio's cheek –
Some dear friend dead, else nothing in the world
Could turn so much the constitution   245
Of any constant man. What, worse and worse?
With leave, Bassanio, I am half yourself,
And I must freely have the half of anything
That this same paper brings you.

BASSANIO

                O sweet Portia,
Here are a few of the unpleasant'st words   250
That ever blotted paper! Gentle lady,
When I did first impart my love to you,

256–7 *Rating myself . . . a braggart:* even in estimating myself so low, I was boasting.
260 *engaged myself:* put myself in debt to.
261 *mere:* absolute.
262 *To feed my means:* to obtain money for me.
263 *as:* i.e. as pale as (the paper is presumably white).
266 *hit:* successfully returned.
270 *merchant-marring:* could refer to merchant ships as well as their owners.
271 *it should appear:* it seems.
272 *present money:* cash in hand.
       discharge: repay.
275 *keen:* sharp, cruel.
276 *plies:* worries, plagues.
277–8 *And doth impeach . . . justice:* attacks the claim of the Venetian state to do equal justice to all who live and work there. Shylock is implicitly claiming that because he is a Jew he is denied his full rights under the law.
279 *magnificoes:* most important citizens of Venice.
280 *port:* distinction and dignity.
281 *envious:* vindictive.

Questions

1 Lines 252–62. How does the disclosure that Bassanio has previously confided the true state of his financial affairs to Portia, before the casket scene, affect one's estimation of his character?

2 How appropriate is Bassanio's image in lines 263–5 to describe Antonio's state?

3 How would you describe the tone of Salerio's speech?

I freely told you all the wealth I had
Ran in my veins – I was a gentleman;
And then I told you true. And yet, dear lady,   255
Rating myself at nothing, you shall see
How much I was a braggart. – When I told you
My state was nothing, I should then have told you
That I was worse than nothing; for indeed
I have engaged myself to a dear friend,   260
Engaged my friend to his mere enemy
To feed my means. Here is a letter, lady;
The paper as the body of my friend,
And every word in it a gaping wound
Issuing life-blood. But is it true, Salerio?   265
Hath *all* his ventures failed? what, not *one* hit?
From Tripolis, from Mexico, and England,
From Lisbon, Barbary, and India,
And not one vessel scape the dreadful touch
Of merchant-marring rocks?

SALERIO

                Not one, my lord.   270
Besides, it should appear that if he had
The present money to discharge the Jew,
He would not take it. Never did I know
A creature that did bear the shape of man
So keen and greedy to confound a man.   275
He plies the duke at morning and at night,
And doth impeach the freedom of the state
If they deny him justice. Twenty merchants,
The duke himself, and the magnificoes
Of greatest port have all persuaded with him,   280
But none can drive him from the envious plea
Of forfeiture, of justice, and his bond.

284 *his countrymen:* i.e. his fellow Jews.
289 *It will go hard:* Antonio will suffer a dreadful fate.
292 *best-conditioned:* best-natured.
293 *courtesies:* good deeds, kindnesses.
294 *The ancient Roman honour:* courage and integrity.
298 *deface:* cancel.
306 *petty:* trifling, unimportant.

Questions

1 What is the significance of Jessica's intervention here and of her words *his countrymen*?
2 What light does Portia's reaction throw upon her character and her feelings for Bassanio?

JESSICA

When I was with him I have heard him swear
To Tubal and to Chus, his countrymen,
That he would rather have Antonio's flesh   285
Than twenty times the value of the sum
That he did owe him. And I know, my lord,
If law, authority, and power deny not,
It will go hard with poor Antonio.

PORTIA

Is it your dear friend that is thus in trouble?   290

BASSANIO

The dearest friend to me, the kindest man,
The best-conditioned and unwearied spirit
In doing courtesies, and one in whom
The ancient Roman honour more appears
Than any that draws breath in Italy.   295

PORTIA

What sum owes he the Jew?

BASSANIO

For me, three thousand ducats.

PORTIA

                      What, no more?
Pay him six thousand, and deface the bond;
Double six thousand, and then treble that,
Before a friend of this description   300
Shall lose a hair through Bassanio's fault.
First go with me to church, and call me wife,
And then away to Venice to your friend;
For never shall you lie by Portia's side
With an unquiet soul. You shall have gold   305
To pay the petty debt twenty times over.

145

309   *maids:* virgins, girls before marriage.
311   *a merry cheer:* a cheerful countenance.
318   *use your pleasure:* do as you wish.
324   *Nor rest . . . us twain:* nor shall sleep come between us (i.e. I shall not sleep until we meet again).

Questions

1 *Since you are dear bought, I will love you dear.* (line 312.) How do you account for Portia's choice of image here? Explain the wordplay involved.

2 What can we learn from the content and style of this letter about the character of Antonio and of his relationship with Bassanio? How does this link with what we already know of Antonio? (See Act 1, Scene 1, and Act 1, Scene 3.)

When it is paid, bring your true friend along. –
My maid Nerissa and myself meantime
Will live as maids and widows. – Come, away!
For you shall hence upon your wedding day.   310
Bid your friends welcome; show a merry cheer –
Since you are dear bought, I will love you dear.
But let me hear the letter of your friend.

BASSANIO (*Reads*)
Sweet Bassanio, my ships have all miscarried, my creditors
grow cruel, my estate is very low, my bond to the Jew is 315
forfeit, and, since in paying it it is impossible I should live,
all debts are cleared between you and I, if I might but see you
at my death. Notwithstanding, use your pleasure; if your
love do not persuade you to come, let not my letter.

PORTIA
O love, dispatch all business and be gone!   320

BASSANIO
Since I have your good leave to go away,
I will make haste; but, till I come again,
No bed shall e'er be guilty of my stay,
Nor rest be interposer 'twixt us twain.

Exeunt

Scene three

Venice. A street.

Enter SHYLOCK *the Jew, with* SOLANIO, *and* ANTONIO, *and a*
GAOLER.

SHYLOCK
Gaoler, look to him; tell not me of mercy;

147

2 *gratis:* freely, without charging interest (or demanding a bond or any kind of security).
9 *fond:* foolish.
14 *dull-eyed:* easily fooled.
16 *intercessors:* pleaders.
18 *it:* he.
    impenetrable: stony-hearted.
19 *kept with:* associated with.
20 *bootless:* useless.

Question

What does Shylock's repeated use of the word *bond* here tell us about him. Contrast the style and tone of his words here with those of his speech to Antonio in Act 1, Scene 3. How do you account for the change?

This is the fool that lent out money gratis.
Gaoler, look to him.

ANTONIO

                      Hear me yet, good Shylock.

SHYLOCK

I'll have my bond; speak not against my bond –
I have sworn an oath that I will have my bond.   5
Thou call'dst me dog before thou hadst a cause,
But since I am a dog, beware my fangs –
The duke shall grant me justice – I do wonder,
Thou naughty gaoler, that thou art so fond
To come abroad with him at his request.   10

ANTONIO

I pray thee hear me speak.

SHYLOCK

I'll have my bond. I will not hear thee speak;
I'll have my bond, and therefore speak no more.
I'll not be made a soft and dull-eyed fool,
To shake the head, relent, and sigh, and yield   15
To Christian intercessors. (*He turns to go*) Follow
   not –
I'll have no speaking; I will have my bond.

                                 Exit

SOLANIO

It is the most impenetrable cur
That ever kept with men.

ANTONIO

                      Let him alone;
I'll follow him no more with bootless prayers.   20
He seeks my life, his reason well I know;

22-3 *I oft delivered . . . moan to me:* I have often helped those who turned to me when they could not repay their debts to him (Shylock).
25 *grant this forfeiture to hold:* allow his bond to be honoured.
27 *commodity:* legal rights.
29 *Will much . . . the state:* will bring into disrepute the reputation of the (Venetian) state for justice to all, natives and strangers alike.
31 *Consisteth of all nations:* the commercial profit of Venice depends on the activities of people of many nationalities. Venice was one of the most important international trading centres in Europe.
32 *bated:* lessened, weakened.

Questions

1 Lines 21–4. How does Antonio account for Shylock's hatred of him and how does this differ from Shylock's own account of his reasons?
2 Lines 26–36. Why, according to Antonio, can the Duke not put himself above the law? Why do you think Antonio urges this reasoning so forcefully?

---

2 *conceit:* understanding, idea.
3 *amity:* friendship.
4 *thus:* in this manner.

I oft delivered from his forfeitures
Many that have at times made moan to me;
Therefore he hates me.

SOLANIO

                    I am sure the duke
Will never grant this forfeiture to hold.   25

ANTONIO

The duke cannot deny the course of law;
For the commodity that strangers have
With us in Venice, if it be denied,
Will much impeach the justice of the state,
Since that the trade and profit of the city   30
Consisteth of all nations. Therefore go. –
These griefs and losses have so bated me
That I shall hardly spare a pound of flesh
To-morrow, to my bloody creditor.
Well gaoler, on. – Pray God Bassanio come   35
To see me pay his debt, and then I care not.

Exeunt

Scene four

Belmont. A room in Portia's house.

Enter PORTIA, NERISSA, LORENZO, JESSICA, *and* BALTHAZAR.

LORENZO

Madam, although I speak it in your presence,
You have a noble and a true conceit
Of god-like amity, which appears most strongly
In bearing thus the absence of your lord.
But if you knew to whom you show this honour,   5

7   *lover:* friend.
9   *Than . . . enforce you:* than even your ordinary generosity would make you.
12 *converse:* associate.
    waste: spend.
13 *Whose souls . . . love:* whose souls bear an equal love for each other.
14 *needs:* of necessity.
14–15 *a like proportion . . . spirit:* be equal in qualities, habits and natures.
17 *bosom lover:* dearest, closest friend.
20 *the semblance of my soul:* the very image of my husband i.e. Antonio.
21 *out:* out of.
25 *husbandary:* daily ordering and running of the household.
33 *imposition:* duty, request.
34 *the which:* which.

Question

Lines 22–3. Why does Portia break off her explanation of her actions here? What was her explanation?

How true a gentleman you send relief,
How dear a lover of my lord your husband,
I know you would be prouder of the work
Than customary bounty can enforce you.

PORTIA

I never did repent for doing good,   10
Nor shall not now; for in companions
That do converse and waste the time together,
Whose souls do bear an egall yoke of love,
There must be needs a like proportion
Of lineaments, of manners, and of spirit;   15
Which makes me think that this Antonio,
Being the bosom lover of my lord,
Must needs be like my lord. If it be so,
How little is the cost I have bestowed
In purchasing the semblance of my soul   20
From out the state of hellish cruelty! –
This comes too near the praising of myself;
Therefore no more of it; hear other things. –
Lorenzo, I commit into your hands
The husbandry and manage of my house,   25
Until my lord's return. For mine own part,
I have toward heaven breathed a secret vow
To live in prayer and contemplation,
Only attended by Nerissa here,
Until her husband and my lord's return.   30
There is a monastery two miles off,
And there we will abide. I do desire you
Not to deny this imposition,
The which my love and some necessity
Now lays upon you.

37 *My people:* my household.
38 *acknowledge:* accept.
49 *Padua:* The University of Padua in northern Italy was famous for its Faculty of Law.
51 *look:* pay close attention to.
52 *imagined:* all imaginable.
53 *traject:* boarding-point for ferry.
54 *trades to:* crosses to.
56 *convenient:* necessary.

Questions
1 What is the dramatic function of this scene between Portia and Lorenzo?
2 What change of mood and tone does Portia display when alone with members of her household after Lorenzo and Jessica have gone?

LORENZO

> Madam, with all my heart, 35
I shall obey you in all fair commands.

PORTIA

My people do already know my mind,
And will acknowledge you and Jessica
In place of Lord Bassanio and myself.
So fare you well till we shall meet again. 40

LORENZO

Fair thoughts and happy hours attend on you!

JESSICA

I wish your ladyship all heart's content.

PORTIA

I thank you for your wish, and am well pleased
To wish it back on you; fare you well, Jessica.

> *Exeunt* JESSICA *and* LORENZO

Now Balthazar, 45
As I have ever found thee honest-true,
So let me find thee still. Take this same letter,
And use thou all th' endeavour of a man
In speed to Padua. See thou render this
Into my cousin's hand, Doctor Bellario, 50
And look what notes and garments he doth give
thee.
Bring them, I pray thee, with imagined speed
Unto the traject, to the common ferry
Which trades to Venice; waste no time in words,
But get thee gone! I shall be there before thee. 55

BALTHAZAR

Madam, I go with all convenient speed.

> *Exit*

60 *habit:* dress.

61 *accomplished:* equipped. Portia is making a bawdy joke about the male costume of the period in which the area covering the crotch, the codpiece, was often emphasized or ornamented (cf. Jessica's embarrassment about being seen dressed as a boy).

62 *that we lack:* that which we lack (i.e. male genitals).
    hold . . . wager: bet you anything you like.

63 *accoutred:* dressed.

65 *braver grace:* more dashing style.

66 *And speak . . . boy:* speak like one whose voice is just breaking.

67 *reed voice:* voice like a reed-pipe.

67–8 *turn two . . . manly stride:* turn my dainty ladylike steps into a man's walk.

68 *frays:* quarrels.

69 *quaint:* elaborate, ingenious.

71 *Which I denying:* which, because I refused them.

72 *I could not do withal:* I could not help it.

74 *puny:* boyish.

77 *bragging Jacks:* raw, youthful, boastful fellows.

80 *If thou wert . . . interpreter:* if you were in the company of someone with a bawdy mind. Portia is referring to the two senses of *turn to men*: (1) turn into or become men (2) take men as lovers.

81 *device:* design, plot.

Questions

1 What effect has this scene on the emotional atmosphere of Act 3?
2 Contrast Portia's manner with Lorenzo and with Nerissa.
3 Why does Portia seem to enjoy her prospective male disguise so much?

PORTIA

    Come on, Nerissa, I have work in hand
    That you yet know not of; we'll see our husbands
    Before they think of us!

NERISSA

                Shall they see us?

PORTIA

    They shall, Nerissa, but in such a habit   60
    That they shall think we are accomplished
    With that we lack. I'll hold thee any wager,
    When we are both accoutered like young men,
    I'll prove the prettier fellow of the two,
    And wear my dagger with the braver grace,   65
    And speak between the change of man and boy,
    With a reed voice, and turn two mincing steps
    Into a manly stride, and speak of frays
    Like a fine bragging youth; and tell quaint lies
    How honourable ladies sought my love,   70
    Which I denying, they fell sick and died.
    I could not do withal. Then I'll repent.
    And wish, for all that, that I had not killed them.
    And twenty of these puny lies I'll tell,
    That men shall swear I have discontinued school   75
    Above a twelvemonth. I have within my mind
    A thousand raw tricks of these bragging Jacks
    Which I will practise.

NERISSA

             Why, shall we turn to men?

PORTIA

    Fie! what a question's that,
    If thou wert near a lewd interpreter!   80
    But come, I'll tell thee all my whole device

82 *stays:* waits.

1 *look you:* note this.
1–2 *the sins ... the children:* Launcelot is quoting from the Bible (*Exodus* 20.5).
3 *fear you:* fear for you.
4 *agitation:* Launcelot could be intending to say 'cogitation' (thoughts) but may simply mean 'anxiety'.
7 *neither:* indeed.
14–15 *Scylla ... Charybdis:* In the Straits of Messina seamen had to pass between the whirlpool of Charybdis and the cave of the sea-monster Scylla.

Question

What is the effect of this scene in which Shylock's servant and his daughter are joking about him at this point in the play?

When I am in my coach, which stays for us
At the park gate; and therefore haste away,
For we must measure twenty miles to-day.

Exeunt

Scene five

Belmont. The garden.

Enter LAUNCELOT *and* JESSICA.

LAUNCELOT
Yes, truly; for look you, the sins of the father are to
be laid upon the children; therefore, I promise you,
I fear you. I was always plain with you, and so now
I speak my agitation of the matter; therefore be of
good cheer, for truly I think you are damned. There   5
is but one hope in it that can do you any good, and
that is but a kind of bastard hope neither.

JESSICA
And what hope is that, I pray thee?

LAUNCELOT
Marry, you may partly hope that your father got
you not, that you are not the Jew's daughter.   10

JESSICA
That were a kind of bastard hope indeed; – so the
sins of my mother should be visited upon me.

LAUNCELOT
Truly, then I fear you are damned both by father
and mother; thus when I shun Scylla, your father, I
fall into Charybdis, your mother; well, you are gone   15
both ways.

17 *I shall be . . . husband:* An allusion to St Paul's saying that 'the misbelieving wife shall be sanctified by her husband' (1 *Corinthians* 7.14). Jessica counters the Old Testament allusion of Launcelot with one from the New Testament of Christianity.

19–20 *we were . . . before:* there are enough of us Christians already.

20–1 *one by another:* together.

22 *pork-eaters:* Christians were not forbidden, like Jews, to eat pork.

23 *rasher on the coals:* bacon grilled (on the coal fire).

29 *are out:* have fallen out.

32 *commonwealth:* state.

36 *the Moor:* we hear no more about this mysterious Moor who seems to be dragged in solely in order that Launcelot may next pun on *Moor* and *more*. The Elizabethans had a greater appetite for puns, serious and humorous, than ourselves!

38 *more than reason:* larger in size than is reasonable.

JESSICA

I shall be saved by my husband; he hath made me a Christian!

LAUNCELOT

Truly, the more to blame he; we were Christians enow before, e'en as many as could well live one by 20 another. This making of Christians will raise the price of hogs – if we grow all to be pork-eaters, we shall not shortly have a rasher on the coals for money.

Enter LORENZO.

JESSICA

I'll tell my husband, Launcelot, what you say; here 25 he comes!

LORENZO

I shall grow jealous of you shortly, Launcelot, if you thus get my wife into corners!

JESSICA

Nay, you need not fear us, Lorenzo; Launcelot and I are out. He tells me flatly there's no mercy for me 30 in heaven, because I am a Jew's daughter; and he says you are no good member of the common-wealth, for in converting Jews to Christians you raise the price of pork.

LORENZO

I shall answer that better to the commonwealth than 35 you can the getting up of the negro's belly; the Moor is with child by you, Launcelot!

LAUNCELOT

It is much that the Moor should be more than reason;

39 *honest:* chaste, faithful.

42–4 *best grace . . . parrots:* wittiest talkers will become silent and only parrots will talk.

45 *stomachs:* appetites.

46 *Goodly:* Gracious.

wit-snapper: player on words, quibbler.

48 *cover:* lay the table. Launcelot deliberately misunderstands the word and takes it to mean 'put one's hat on' in reply to Lorenzo's question.

51 *quarrelling with occasion:* seizing every chance to argue and quibble.

56 *For:* as for. By *table*, Launcelot here means the meal itself.

57 *covered:* served in covered dishes.

58 *humours and conceits:* your wishes and inclinations.

Questions

1 How should Lorenzo be played in this scene, in your opinion?

2 What light does this scene throw upon Launcelot's relationship with Jessica? What bearing does this have on their tearful farewell to each other in Act 2, Scene 3?

but if she be less than an honest woman, she is indeed
more than I took her for.   40

LORENZO
How every fool can play upon the word! I think the
best grace of wit will shortly turn into silence, and
discourse grow commendable in none only but parrots. – Go in, sirrah; bid them prepare for dinner!

LAUNCELOT
That is done, sir; they have all stomachs!   45

LORENZO
Goodly Lord, what a wit-snapper are you! then bid
them prepare dinner!

LAUNCELOT
That is done too, sir, only "cover" is the word.

LORENZO
Will you cover then, sir?

LAUNCELOT
Not so, sir, neither; I know my duty.   50

LORENZO
Yet more quarrelling with occasion! Wilt thou show
the whole wealth of thy wit in an instant? I pray
thee understand a plain man in his plain meaning:
go to thy fellows, bid them cover the table, serve in
the meat, and we will come in to dinner.   55

LAUNCELOT
For the table, sir, it shall be served in; for the meat,
sir, it shall be covered. For your coming in to dinner, sir, why, let it be as humours and conceits shall
govern.

Exit

60 *dear discretion:* Lorenzo exclaims on Launcelot's jokes which are very contrived, and comments on how dearly bought or precious is true judgement or discernment in speech.
suited: twisted to fit the occasion.

61 *fool:* clown.

63 *A many:* many.
that stand in better place: who have higher positions.

64 *Garnished like him:* possessed of a similar vocabulary of *good words.*
for a tricksy word: for the sake of an ingenious piece of word-play.

65 *Defy the matter:* pay no attention to the actual sense.
How cheers't thou?: How are you?

68 *meet:* suitable.

69 *live:* should live.

70–3 *For, having . . . heaven:* If Bassanio does not live the upright life which he does, then Portia would be sufficient blessing for him here on earth and he would not deserve any further reward in heaven.

77 *Pawned:* wagered (along with the other).
rude: primitive.

78 *fellow:* equal.

82 *stomach:* (1) inclination (2) appetite.

Question

What is the effect of Jessica's words about Portia on our impression of both ladies?

LORENZO

O dear discretion, how his words are suited!   60
The fool hath planted in his memory
An army of good words, and I do know
A many fools that stand in better place,
Garnished like him, that for a tricksy word
Defy the matter. How cheer'st thou, Jessica?   65
And now, good sweet, say thy opinion,
How dost thou like the Lord Bassanio's wife?

JESSICA

Past all expressing; it is very meet
The Lord Bassanio live an upright life
For, having such a blessing in his lady,   70
He finds the joys of heaven here on earth,
And if on earth he do not merit it,
In reason he should never come to heaven!
Why, if two gods should play some heavenly match,
And on the wager lay two earthly women,   75
And Portia one, there must be something else
Pawned with the other, for the poor rude world
Hath not her fellow.

LORENZO

                Even such a husband
Hast thou of me, as she is for a wife.

JESSICA

Nay, but ask my opinion too of that.   80

LORENZO

I will anon; first, let us go to dinner.

JESSICA

Nay, let me praise you while I have a stomach.

84 *howsome'er:* in whatever way.
85 *set you forth:* (1) praise you (2) set the meal before you.

Questions

1 Why do you think Act 3 ends on a lighthearted note with the lovers, Lorenzo and Jessica, leaving the stage last?
2 Trace the dramatic climaxes, the high points of feeling, in this act.

ACT THREE SCENE FIVE

LORENZO

No, pray thee, let it serve for table-talk;
Then, howsome'er thou speak'st, 'mong other things
I shall digest it.

JESSICA

             Well, I'll set you forth.   85

                            Exeunt

6 *from any dram:* of the smallest drop.
7 *qualify:* soften, moderate.
8 *stands obdurate:* remains unmoved.
9 *that:* because.
10 *his envy's reach:* the reach of his malice.
13 *the very tyranny:* the utmost force.

Questions

1 What has Antonio resolved to do?
2 What is the significance of the Duke's manner of referring to Shylock?

Act Four

Scene one

Venice. A Court of Justice.

Enter the DUKE, *the Magnificoes* ANTONIO, BASSANIO, *and* GRATIANO, SALERIO *and others.*

DUKE

What, is Antonio here?

ANTONIO

Ready, so please your grace!

DUKE

I am sorry for thee; thou art come to answer
A stony adversary, an inhuman wretch,
Uncapable of pity, void and empty   5
From any dram of mercy.

ANTONIO

                I have heard
Your grace hath ta'en great pains to qualify
His rigorous course; but since he stands obdurate,
And that no lawful means can carry me
Out of his envy's reach, I do oppose   10
My patience to his fury, and am armed
To suffer with a quietness of spirit
The very tyranny and rage of his.

DUKE

Go, one, call the Jew into the court.

SALERIO

He is ready at the door; he comes, my lord.   15

169

18 *leadest this fashion:* display this outward show.
19 *the last hour of act:* the very last moment.
20 *remorse:* pity or compassion.
21 *strange:* remarkable.
22 *where:* whereas.
24 *loose the forfeiture:* cancel the bond.
26 *a moiety of the principal:* part of the capital lent; 'moiety' now means 'half'.
31 *From ... flints:* command pity for his situation from hearts as unfeeling as brass and hard as stone.
32 *stubborn:* unmoved, without pity. Turks and Tartars had a reputation for cruelty.
33 *offices:* practices.
34 *gentle:* merciful, the possible pun on 'gentle' throws back on Shylock, a reminder of his religion which ought to make him merciful if he is a religious man.
35 *possessed:* informed.
    purpose: intend.
37 *due:* what is legally owed to me.
38 *light:* alight, come down on.
43 *my humour:* my whim.

Questions

1 What alternative plan does the Duke credit Shylock with and what is his motive? How does the word *act* function within the logic of his speech?
2 Why should the Duke make a contrastive reference to Turks and Tartars in demanding mercy from Shylock?
3 Why do you think Shylock has the audacity to speak lines 38 and 39 to the Duke in this assembly?

Enter SHYLOCK.

DUKE

    Make room, and let him stand before our face.
    Shylock, the world thinks, and I think so too,
    That thou but leadest this fashion of thy malice
    To the last hour of act, and then 't is thought
    Thou'lt show thy mercy and remorse, more strange 20
    Than is thy strange apparent cruelty;
    And where thou now exact'st the penalty,
    Which is a pound of this poor merchant's flesh,
    Thou wilt not only loose the forfeiture,
    But, touched with human gentleness and love,   25
    Forgive a moiety of the principal,
    Glancing an eye of pity on his losses
    That have of late so huddled on his back
    Enow to press a royal merchant down,
    And pluck commiseration of his state   30
    From brassy bosoms and rough hearts of flint,
    From stubborn Turks, and Tartars never trained
    To offices of tender courtesy.
    We all expect a gentle answer, Jew!

SHYLOCK

    I have possessed your grace of what I purpose,   35
    And by our holy Sabbath have I sworn
    To have the due and forfeit of my bond.
    If you deny it, let the danger light
    Upon your charter and your city's freedom!
    You'll ask me why I rather choose to have   40
    A weight of carrion flesh than to receive
    Three thousand ducats. I'll not answer that!
    But say it is my humour – is it answered?
    What if my house be troubled with a rat,
    And I be pleased to give ten thousand ducats   45

46 *ban'd:* poisoned.
47 *gaping pig:* a boar's head on a dish, often served with a fruit stuck in the open mouth, considered a great delicacy.
49 *sings i' the' nose:* sound its nasal notes.
50 *affection:* desire(s).
51 *passions:* emotions. Shylock's meaning is that a person's feelings are controlled by deeper desires and impulses (than can be explained).
56 *of force:* of necessity.
58 *As to ... being offended:* reacting in an offensive manner to what has offended or disgusted him.
60 *lodged:* firm, fixed.
    certain: particular.
62 *losing suit:* i.e. one in which Shylock stands to lose money. There is a certain irony in the phrase.
64 *current:* flow.

Questions

1 Why does Shylock not mention the reasons for hating Antonio which he has already given?

2 Why do you think Shylock speaks in blank verse rather than in prose in this speech? What pattern can you find in his switching modes of speech in the scenes which have preceded this one?

3 What does the exchange of words between Bassanio and Shylock tell us about both of them at this point?

To have it baned? – what, are you answered yet?
Some men there are love not a gaping pig;
Some that are mad if they behold a cat;
And others, when the bagpipe sings i' the' nose,
Cannot contain their urine – for affection,   50
Master of passion, sways it to the mood
Of what it likes or loathes. Now for your answer:
As there is no firm reason to be rendered
Why *he* cannot abide a gaping pig,
Why *he* a harmless, necessary cat,   55
Why *he* a woollen bagpipe, but of force
Must yield to such inevitable shame
As to offend, himself being offended;
So can I give no reason, nor I will not,
More than a lodged hate and a certain loathing   60
I bear Antonio, that I follow thus
A losing suit against him! – Are you answered?

BASSANIO

This is no answer, thou unfeeling man,
To excuse the current of thy cruelty.

SHYLOCK

I am not bound to please thee with my answers!   65

BASSANIO

Do all men kill the things they do not love?

SHYLOCK

Hates any man the thing he would not kill?

BASSANIO

Every offence is not a hate at first!

SHYLOCK

What! wouldst thou have a serpent sting thee twice?

173

70 *think you:* bear in mind (that it is Shylock you are dealing with).
72 *bid the . . . height:* command the tide of the sea to fall below its usual level.
77 *fretten:* fretted, agitated.
82 *with all . . . conveniency:* as quickly and directly as possible.
87 *draw:* take.
92 *abject and in slavish parts:* menial duties.
95 *burthens:* burdens.
96-7 *let their . . . viands:* let their tastes become accustomed to such foods.

Questions

1 Lines 70–83. How far does Antonio's speech match his intention expressed in his earlier words to the Duke?
2 What is implied in Antonio's choice and use of imagery in this speech?
3 How does Antonio's speech bear out some of what Shylock has accused him of?

ANTONIO

I pray you think you question with the Jew.   70
You may as well go stand upon the beach
And bid the main flood bate his usual height;
You may as well use question with the wolf,
Why he hath made the ewe bleat for the lamb;
You may as well forbid the mountain pines   75
To wag their high tops, and to make no noise
When they are fretten with the gusts of heaven;
You may as well do anything most hard
As seek to soften that – than which what's harder? –
His Jewish heart! Therefore, I do beseech you,   80
Make no more offers, use no farther means,
But with all brief and plain conveniency
Let me have judgement, and the Jew his will!

BASSANIO

For thy three thousand ducats, here is six!

SHYLOCK

If every ducat in six thousand ducats   85
Were in six parts, and every part a ducat,
I would not draw them; I would have my bond!

DUKE

How shalt thou hope for mercy, rendering none?

SHYLOCK

What judgement shall I dread, doing no wrong?
You have among you many a purchased slave,   90
Which, like your asses, and your dogs and mules,
You use in abject and in slavish parts,
Because you bought them; shall I say to you,
Let them be free, marry them to your heirs?
Why sweat they under burthens? let their beds   95
Be made as soft as yours, and let their palates

101 *fie upon:* down with.
104 *Upon my power:* by my authority.
105 *doctor:* doctor of law, an academic title.
107 *stays without:* waits outside.
114 *tainted wether:* a diseased ram.
115 *Meetest:* fittest.
118 *epitaph:* funeral speech or inscription upon a tomb.

Questions

1 Show how Shylock counters every attempt to persuade him to change his mind. Do you find his arguments convincing?
2 Lines 114–18. How do you account for Antonio's response to Bassanio's attempt to hearten him in lines 111–13?
3 Lines 104–7. Why do you think the Duke threatens to dismiss the court?

Be seasoned with such viands? You will answer
"The slaves are ours." – So do I answer you:
The pound of flesh which I demand of him
Is dearly bought, 't is mine and I will have it;   100
If you deny me, fie upon your law!
There is no force in the decrees of Venice!
I stand for judgement; answer, shall I have it?

DUKE

Upon my power I may dismiss this court,
Unless Bellario, a learned doctor,   105
Whom I have sent for to determine this,
Come here to-day.

SALERIO

                    My lord, here stays without
A messenger with letters from the doctor,
New come from Padua.

DUKE

Bring us the letters! call the messenger!   110

BASSANIO

Good cheer, Antonio! what, man, courage yet!
The Jew shall have my flesh, blood, bones and all,
Ere thou shalt lose for me one drop of blood.

ANTONIO

I am a tainted wether of the flock,
Meetest for death; the weakest kind of fruit   115
Drops earliest to the ground, and so let me;
You cannot better be employed, Bassanio,
Than to live still and write mine epitaph.

Enter NERISSA, *dressed like a lawyer's clerk.*

DUKE

Came you from Padua, from Bellario?

121 *whet:* sharpen.
122 *the forfeiture:* i.e. the pound of flesh from Antonio's body.
124–6 *no metal . . . envy:* no metal can cut more sharply than the edge of your hatred.
128 *inexorable:* unyielding.
129 *for thy life . . . accused:* justice itself must be at fault if you are allowed to live.
130 *waver in my faith:* shake my Christian belief.
131 *to hold opinion:* to agree.
     Pythagoras: an ancient Greek philosopher who held the belief that souls pass from animals to men.
133 *trunks:* bodies.
     currish: bestial, like a dog's.
135 *fell:* savage.
     fleet: fly away.
136 *unhallowed:* unholy, accursed.
     dam: used to denote the mother of an animal.
137 *Infused itself:* poured itself.
138 *starved:* murderous.
139 *rail . . . my bond:* take the seal off my bond with your verbal attacks.
140 *offend'st:* harm.
141 *wit:* reasoning power.
142 *cureless ruin:* incurable damage.

Question

Describe how the tension mounts at this point. What part does Gratiano play in heightening it?

178

NERISSA

From both, my lord. Bellario greets your grace.   120

She gives him a letter.

BASSANIO

Why dost thou whet thy knife so earnestly?

SHYLOCK

To cut the forfeiture from that bankrupt there!

GRATIANO

Not on thy sole, but on thy soul, harsh Jew,
Thou mak'st thy knife keen; but no metal can,
No, not the hangman's axe, bear half the keenness 125
Of thy sharp envy. Can no prayers pierce thee?

SHYLOCK

No, none that *thou* hast wit enough to make.

GRATIANO

O, be thou damned, inexorable dog!
And for thy life let justice be accused;
Thou almost mak'st me waver in my faith   130
To hold opinion with Pythagoras,
That souls of animals infuse themselves
Into the trunks of men: thy currish spirit
Governed a wolf, who, hanged for human slaughter,
Even from the gallows did his fell soul fleet,   135
And, whilst thou layest in thy unhallowed dam,
Infused itself in thee; for thy desires
Are wolvish, bloody, starved, and ravenous.

SHYLOCK

Till thou canst rail the seal from off my bond,
Thou but offend'st thy lungs to speak so loud;   140
Repair thy wit, good youth, or it will fall
To cureless ruin. I stand here for law.

145 *hard by:* nearby.
152 *in loving visitation:* paying a friendly visit.
156 *bettered:* improved.
158 *importunity:* earnest request.
     in my stead: in my place.
159–60 *I beseech you . . . estimation:* I ask you not to let his youth prevent him from being highly respected.
162 *whose trial . . . commendation:* when he is tested, he will more than live up to my praise.

Questions

1 Explain why you think Bellario has taken the risk of sending Portia/Balthazar in his place?

2 What does his commendation add to our estimation of Portia?

Note: Portia, though recognizable to the audience, will not be recognized by Bassanio and the others according to a convention of the Elizabethan stage where deliberately disguised characters were accepted as their assumed personalities even by those who were related to them.

DUKE

This letter from Bellario doth commend
A young and learned doctor to our court.
Where is he?

NERISSA

He attendeth here hard by   145
To know your answer, whether you'll admit him.

DUKE

With all my heart; some three or four of you
Go give him courteous conduct to this place;
Meantime the court shall hear Bellario's letter.
(*Reads*) *Your grace shall understand that at the receipt of* 150
your letter I am very sick, but in the instant that your messen-
ger came, in loving visitation was with me a young doctor of
Rome; his name is Balthazar. I acquainted him with the
cause in controversy between the Jew and Antonio the mer-
chant; we turned o'er many books together; he is furnished 155
with my opinion, which, bettered with his own learning, the
greatness whereof I cannot enough commend, comes with him
at my importunity, to fill up your grace's request in my stead.
I beseech you let his lack of years be no impediment to let him
lack a reverend estimation, for I never knew so young a body 160
with so old a head. I leave him to your gracious acceptance,
whose trial shall better publish his commendation.

Enter PORTIA, *dressed as* BALTHAZAR, *a doctor of laws.*

You hear the learn'd Bellario what he writes,
(*He sees* PORTIA) And here, I take it, is the doctor
  come.
(*To* PORTIA) Give me your hand. Came you from old
  Bellario?   165

PORTIA

I did, my lord.

181

167   *difference:* dispute.
168   *holds this present question:* is the cause of the present case.
169   *throughly:* thoroughly.
174   *in such rule:* so clearly according to law.
175   *impugn:* find fault with.
176   *within his danger:* in his power.
177   *confess:* admit.
178   *must:* Portia does not mean that Shylock is legally obliged to show mercy but that, like any ordinary human being, he will 'of course' be merciful. Shylock deliberately misunderstands her when he repeats *must* in his question.

Questions

1 Why does Portia ask the question in line 170?
2 How should Portia act the role of Balthazar in this scene?

DUKE

You are welcome; take your place;
Are you acquainted with the difference
That holds this present question in the court?

PORTIA

I am informèd throughly of the cause.
Which is the merchant here? and which the Jew? 170

DUKE

Antonio and old Shylock, both stand forth.

PORTIA

Is your name Shylock?

SHYLOCK

Shylock is my name.

PORTIA

Of a strange nature is the suit you follow,
Yet in such rule that the Venetian law
Cannot impugn you as you do proceed. 175
(*To* ANTONIO) You stand within his danger, do you
not?

ANTONIO

Ay, so he says.

PORTIA

Do you confess the bond?

ANTONIO

I do.

PORTIA

Then must the Jew be merciful.

SHYLOCK

On what compulsion must I? tell me that.

183

180 *strained:* constrained. No one is compelled to be merciful.
184 *mightiest:* strongest.
    becomes: suits.
186 *temporal power:* earthly, as opposed to spiritual, power.
186 *attribute to:* characteristic of.
192 *show likest:* most resemble.
193 *When mercy seasons justice:* when mercy is added to justice.
195–6 *in the course . . . see salvation:* if strict justice alone were observed, no man would be saved since all men are sinners.
196–8 *we do pray . . . the deeds of mercy:* as we pray for mercy,: we should show it to others. cf. The Lord's Prayer: 'Forgive us our trespasses as we forgive them that trespass against us.'
199 *mitigate:* moderate.
202 *My deeds upon my head:* let me be responsible for the consequences of my own actions.
    crave: appeal to.
204 *discharge:* repay.
205 *tender:* offer.

Questions

1 What are the arguments used by Portia in favour of mercy?
2 Why should her speech evoke no response from Shylock?

PORTIA
    The quality of mercy is not strained;   180
    It droppeth as the gentle rain from heaven
    Upon the place beneath; it is twice blest:
    It blesseth him that gives, and him that takes;
    'T is mightiest in the mightiest; it becomes
    The thronèd monarch better than his crown.   185
    His sceptre shows the force of temporal power,
    The attribute to awe and majesty,
    Wherein doth sit the dread and fear of kings;
    But mercy is above this sceptred sway;
    It is enthronèd in the nearts of kings;   190
    It is an attribute to God himself;
    And earthly power doth then show likest God's
    When mercy seasons justice. Therefore, Jew,
    Though justice be thy plea, consider this,
    That in the course of justice none of us   195
    Should see salvation; we do pray for mercy,
    And that same prayer doth teach us all to render
    The deeds of mercy. I have spoke thus much
    To mitigate the justice of thy plea,
    Which, if thou follow, this strict court of Venice   200
    Must needs give sentence 'gainst the merchant there.

SHYLOCK
    My deeds upon my head! I crave the law,
    The penalty and forfeit of my bond.

PORTIA
    Is he not able to discharge the money?

BASSANIO
    Yes, here I tender it for him in the court;   205
    Yea, twice the sum; if that will not suffice,

210 *malice ... truth:* (Shylock's) hatred stands in the way of fair dealing.
211 *Wrest once the law:* just this one time, bend the law.
213 *curb:* restrain.
216 *for:* as.
      precedent: an earlier judgement which must be followed in other cases
      of a similar kind.
217 *error:* wrong judgement.
219 *Daniel:* Daniel was a wise judge who, as a young man, saved Susanna
      from false accusation by the Elders of Israel. The name Daniel means
      'God is my judge' in Hebrew.
225 *perjury:* to be false to an oath. Shylock means that to commit the sin of
      perjury would injure his soul.

Questions

1 Why is Shylock so excited over Portia's speech in lines 214–18?
2 How have his tone and bearing changed?
3 What methods have been used to induce Shylock to change his mind
   from the beginning of this scene?

I will be bound to pay it ten times o'er
On forfeit of my hands, my head, my heart;
If this will not suffice, it must appear
That malice bears down truth. And I beseech you 210
Wrest once the law to your authority;
To do a great right, do a little wrong,
And curb this cruel devil of his will.

PORTIA

It must not be; there is no power in Venice
Can alter a decree establishèd;   215
'T will be recorded for a precedent,
And many an error by the same example
Will rush into the state. It cannot be:

SHYLOCK

A Daniel come to judgement! yea, a Daniel!
O wise young judge, how I do honour thee!   220

PORTIA

I pray you let me look upon the bond.

SHYLOCK

Here 't is, most reverend doctor, here it is.

PORTIA

Shylock, there's thrice thy money offered thee.

SHYLOCK

An oath, an oath, I have an oath in heaven. –
Shall I lay perjury upon my soul?   225
No, not for Venice.

PORTIA

Why, this bond is forfeit,
And lawfully by this the Jew may claim
A pound of flesh, to be by him cut off

231 *tenor:* terms.
233 *exposition:* interpretation.
238 *I stay here:* I take my stand.
244 *Hath full relation to:* is in full agreement with.
247 *more elder:* older.

Questions

1 How should Portia play out her role as Balthazar at this point in the scene?
2 Explain why Antonio speaks on in lines 239–40.
3 What are our feelings towards Shylock in this scene and at this point in particular?

Nearest the merchant's heart. (*To* SHYLOCK) Be
   merciful,
Take thrice thy money; bid me tear the bond.   230

SHYLOCK

When it is paid, according to the tenor.
It doth appear you are a worthy judge,
You know the law; your exposition
Hath been most sound. I charge you by the law,
Whereof you are a well-deserving pillar,   235
Proceed to judgement; by my soul I swear,
There is no power in the tongue of man
To alter me. I stay here on my bond.

ANTONIO

Most heartily I do beseech the court
To give the judgement.

PORTIA

                                    Why then thus it is: 240
You must prepare your bosom for his knife.

SHYLOCK

O noble judge! O excellent young man!

PORTIA

For the intent and purpose of the law
Hath full relation to the penalty,
Which here appeareth due upon the bond.   245

SHYLOCK

'T is very true. O wise and upright judge,
How much more elder art thou than thy looks!

PORTIA

(*To* ANTONIO) Therefore, lay bare your bosom.

251 *balance:* a pair of scales.
253 *on your charge:* at your expense.
255 *nominated:* set out.
264 *use:* practice.

Questions

1 Lines 253–4. Why does Portia give this order to Shylock?
2 What does Shylock's answer tell us about his attitude?
3 Why does Antonio address Bassanio rather than the court or Portia?

SHYLOCK

                              Ay, his breast,
So says the bond, doth it not, noble judge?
"Nearest his heart", those are the very words.   250

PORTIA

It is so. Are there balance here to weigh
The flesh?

SHYLOCK

              I have them ready.

PORTIA

Have by some surgeon, Shylock, on your charge,
To stop his wounds, lest he do bleed to death.

SHYLOCK

Is it so nominated in the bond?   255

PORTIA

It is not so expressed, but what of that?
'T were good you do so much for charity.

SIIYLOCK

I cannot find it; 't is not in the bond.

PORTIA

(*To* ANTONIO) You merchant, have you anything to
    say?

ANTONIO

But little. I am armed and well prepared.   260
Give me your hand, Bassanio; fare you well,
Grieve not that I am fall'n to this for you,
For herein Fortune shows herself more kind
Than is her custom. It is still her use
To let the wretched man outlive this wealth,   265
To view with hollow eye and wrinkled brow

270   *process:* course.
271   *speak me fair:* speak well of me.
273   *a love:* a true friend.
274–5 *Repent but you . . . repents not:* so long as you feel some sorrow at losing
      your friend, he will have no regrets.
277   *with all my heart:* Antonio puns on the literal and figurative meanings
      of this phrase.
286   *protest:* declare.
290   *else:* otherwise.

Questions

1 Lines 260–77. What fresh light does Antonio's speech throw upon
  his feelings for Bassanio?
2 How does our knowledge of Portia's real identify affect our response
  to the situation?
3 Lines 284–5. What effect do these lines have on the atmosphere of
  the scene at this point?
4 Looking back over Antonio's previous appearances and speeches,
  can you detect any pattern of consistency which is rounded off by
  this speech at this point in the play?
5 *These be the Christian husbands!* (line 291). How should Shylock speak
  this line? What does he mean by this exclamation and what effect
  does it have on our response to the situation?

An age of poverty: from which ling'ring penance
Of such misery doth she cut me off.
Commend me to your honourable wife;
Tell her the process of Antonio's end,   270
Say how I loved you, speak me fair in death;
And when the tale is told, bid her be judge
Whether Bassanio had not once a love;
Repent but you that you shall lose your friend
And he repents not that he pays your debt.   275
For if the Jew do cut but deep enough,
I'll pay it instantly, with all my heart.

BASSANIO
Antonio, I am married to a wife
Which is as dear to me as life itself,
But life itself, my wife, and all the world,   280
Are not with me esteemed above thy life.
I would lose all, ay, sacrifice them all
Here to this devil, to deliver you.

PORTIA
Your wife would give you little thanks for that
If she were by to hear you make the offer.   285

GRATIANO
I have a wife who I protest I love –
I would she were in heaven, so she could
Entreat some power to change this currish Jew.

NERISSA
'T is well you offer it behind her back;
The wish would make else an unquiet house.   290

SHYLOCK (*Aside*)
These be the Christian husbands! I have a
    daughter –

193

292-3 *Would any . . . husband:* I would rather she had married any descendant of Barabbas (a Jewish criminal who was pardoned instead of Christ) rather than a Christian.
294 *trifle:* waste.
301 *Tarry:* wait.
302 *jot:* drop.
307 *confiscate:* forfeit.
310 *Thyself:* you yourself.

Questions

1 How does Shylock's recollection of his daughter affect our view of him?
2 Line 299. What is the effect of this repetition by Portia?
3 How is it that Shylock has permitted himself to fall into Portia's trap, in your view?
4 Do you think that Portia acts out of premeditation -- that she has come to court prepared for this moment - or that the solution has come to her in the course of the preceding action? What evidence would you use to defend your judgement here?

Would any of the stock of Barabbas
Had been her husband, rather than a Christian.
(*Aloud*) We trifle time; I pray thee pursue sentence.

PORTIA

A pound of that same merchant's flesh is thine;   295
The court awards it, and the law doth give it.

SHYLOCK

Most rightful judge!

PORTIA

And you must cut this flesh from off his breast;
The law allows it, and the court awards it.

SHYLOCK

Most learned judge! A sentence! Come, prepare!   300

PORTIA

Tarry a little; there is something else:
This bond doth give thee here no jot of blood;
The words expressly are "a pound of flesh";
Take then thy bond, take thou thy pound of flesh,
But in the cutting it, if thou dost shed   305
One drop of Christian blood, thy lands and goods
Are (by the laws of Venice) confiscate
Unto the state of Venice.

GRATIANO

                    O upright judge! –
Mark, Jew – O learned judge!

SHYLOCK

Is that the law?

PORTIA

                    Thyself shalt see the act;   310
For as thou urgest justice, be assured

316   *Soft!:* Just a moment!
317   *all justice:* only justice, nothing more.
323   *a just pound:* exactly a pound, no more, no less.
325–6 *the division . . . scruple:* A scruple is a small weight equal to 20 grains; these weights are used in measuring medicine.
327   *estimation:* amount.
330   *on the hip:* at a disadvantage. (Recall Shylock's earlier use of the phrase in Act 1, Scene 3, line 41.)

Questions

1 Lines 311–12, 316–18 and 320–8. How does our knowledge of Portia up to this point in the play prepare us for her firmness in this scene and in these speeches?
2 What is the dramatic function of Gratiano's comments here?

Thou shalt have justice more than thou desir'st.

GRATIANO

O learned judge! – Mark, Jew, a learned judge!

SHYLOCK

I take this offer then; pay the bond thrice,
And let the Christian go.

BASSANIO

Here is the money.   315

PORTIA

Soft!
The Jew shall have all justice; soft, no haste!
He shall have nothing but the penalty.

GRATIANO

O Jew! an upright judge, a learned judge!

PORTIA

Therefore prepare thee to cut off the flesh;   320
Shed thou no blood, nor cut thou less nor more
But just a pound of flesh. If thou tak'st more
Or less than a just pound, be it but so much
As makes it light or heavy in the substance
Or the division of the twentieth part   325
Of one poor scruple – nay, if the scale do turn
But in the estimation of a hair,
Thou diest, and all thy goods are confiscate.

GRATIANO

A second Daniel, A Daniel, Jew! –
Now, infidel, I have you on the hip.   330

PORTIA

Why doth the Jew pause? (*To* SHYLOCK) Take thy
    forfeiture.

332 *principal:* original sum lent.
338 *barely:* only.
342 *I'll stay . . . question:* I'll not wait to argue any longer.
348 *'gainst the which:* against whom.
    contrive: plot.
350 *privy coffer:* private (i.e. the Duke's) treasury.
351 *in:* at.
352 *'gainst all other voice:* without regard to any other appeals. Only the Duke
    could pardon the offender.

Questions

1 What contrasts in character are provided by each of the speakers
in this part of the scene?
2 How do these affect the emotional atmosphere and the pace of the
scene?

SHYLOCK

Give me my principal, and let me go.

BASSANIO

I have it ready for thee; here it is.

PORTIA

He hath refused it in the open court;
He shall have merely justice and his bond.   335

GRATIANO

A Daniel still say I, a second Daniel!
I thank thee Jew for teaching me that word.

SHYLOCK

Shall I not have barely my principal?

PORTIA

Thou shalt have nothing but the forfeiture,
To be so taken at thy peril, Jew.   340

SHYLOCK

Why then, the devil give him good of it;
I'll stay no longer question.

PORTIA

                    Tarry, Jew;
The law hath yet another hold on you.
It is enacted in the laws of Venice,
If it be proved against an alien   345
That by direct or indirect attempts
He seek the life of any citizen,
The party 'gainst the which he doth contrive,
Shall seize one half his goods; the other half
Comes to the privy coffer of the state,   350
And the offender's life lies in the mercy
Of the Duke only, 'gainst all other voice.

THE MERCHANT OF VENICE

354   *For it . . . proceeding:* it is perfectly clear from your actions.
357–8 *thou hast incurred . . . rehearsed:* you have put yourself within the scope
      of the law I have just mentioned.
362   *cord:* a rope to be hanged with.
364   *That:* in order that.
366   *For:* as for.
368   *Which . . . a fine:* if you repent sufficiently I may alter it (i.e. confis-
      cation of half his wealth) into a fine.
369   *for . . . Antonio:* Portia insists that any reduction in the penalty
      imposed on Shylock should be made only in that portion of his wealth
      due to the state, not to Antonio.
375   *a halter:* hangman's noose.
      gratis: free.

Questions

1 What is *the difference of our spirit* which the Duke speaks of in line
  364?
2 Why do you think that the Duke is capable of being so magnani-
  mous to Shylock?
3 How do you account for Portia's insistence on Shylock's paying as
  much of the penalty as the Duke will permit?
4 How far do Gratiano's interventions affect our feelings towards
  Shylock at this point. How much are you in sympathy with
  Gratiano's point of view?

In which predicament I say thou stand'st;
For it appears by manifest proceeding,
That indirectly, and directly too,   355
Thou hast contrived against the very life
Of the defendant; and thou hast incurred
The danger formerly by me rehearsed.
Down, therefore, and beg mercy of the duke.

GRATIANO

Beg that thou may'st have leave to hang thyself.   360
And yet, thy wealth being forfeit to the state,
Thou hast not left the value of a cord;
Therefore thou must be hanged at the state's
    charge.

DUKE

That thou shalt see the difference of our spirit,
I pardon thee thy life before thou ask it;   365
For half thy wealth, it is Antonio's,
The other half comes to the general state,
Which humbleness may drive unto a fine.

PORTIA

Ay, for the state, not for Antonio.

SHYLOCK

Nay, take my life and all, pardon not that.   370
You take my house when you do take the prop
That doth sustain my house; you take my life
When you do take the means whereby I live.

PORTIA

What mercy can you render him, Antonio?

GRATIANO

A halter gratis; nothing else, for God's sake!   375

376 *So please:* if it pleases.
377 *quit:* cancel.
378 *so:* on condition that.
379 *in use:* in trust.
382 *Two things provided more:* provided that two more conditions are fulfilled.
384 *record a gift:* sign a legal document bequeathing his property.
394–6 Instead of the two godfathers you should normally have at your christening, I wish you had ten more (meaning the twelve members of a jury) who would pass sentence of death on you rather than baptize you. 'Godfathers' was a slang term for members of a jury.

Questions

1 Lines 376–86. What is characteristic about Antonio's proposition to the court and the Duke with regard to the punishment of Shylock?
2 How do you feel about Shylock as he leaves the stage?

ANTONIO

So please my lord the Duke and all the court
To quit the fine for one half of his goods,
I am content; so he will let me have
The other half in use, to render it
Upon his death unto the gentleman   380
That lately stole his daughter.
Two things provided more, – that for this
   favour
He presently become a Christian;
The other, that he do record a gift,
Here in the court, of all he dies possessed   385
Unto his son Lorenzo and his daughter.

DUKE

He shall do this, or else I do recant
The pardon that I late pronouncèd here.

PORTIA

Art thou contented, Jew? What dost thou say?

SHYLOCK

I am content.

PORTIA

            Clerk, draw a deed of gift.   390

SHYLOCK

I pray you give me leave to go from hence;
I am not well; send the deed after me,
And I will sign it.

DUKE

            Get thee gone, but do it.

GRATIANO

In christening shalt thou have two godfathers;

203

397 *entreat:* desire.
400 *meet:* fitting, necessary.
402 *gratify:* show your gratitude (by rewarding him well).
403 *bound:* indebted (perhaps with a joking reference to the very different 'bind' Shylock mentions).
406 *in lieu whereof:* in place of which.
408 *cope:* reward.
414 *My mind . . . mercenary:* I have never been concerned to make money.
415 Portia is making a private joke which the audience, but not Antonio or Bassanio, can share.

Questions

1 *Exit Shylock.* In one Stratford production, Shylock, who had been wearing a pointed yellow cap as a 'badge' of his Jewishness imposed on him as an alien, takes it off just before he exits. It is left behind on the stage. What would be the dramatic purpose of such a symbolic gesture at this point?

2 How does Gratiano's attitude to Shylock differ from that of Portia, Antonio, Bassanio and the Duke? What is the dramatic significance of this character in the Trial Scene?

Had I been judge, thou shouldst have had ten more, 395
To bring thee to the gallows, not to the font.

Exit SHYLOCK

DUKE

Sir, I entreat you home with me to dinner.

PORTIA

I humbly do desire your grace of pardon;
I must away this night toward Padua,
And it is meet I presently set forth.   400

DUKE

I am sorry that your leisure serves you not.
Antonio, gratify this gentleman,
For in my mind you are much bound to him.

Exit DUKE *and his train*

BASSANIO

Most worthy gentleman, I and my friend
Have by your wisdom been this day acquitted   405
Of grievous penalties, in lieu whereof,
Three thousand ducats due unto the Jew
We freely cope your courteous pains withal.

ANTONIO

And stand indebted over and above
In love and service to you evermore.   410

PORTIA

He is well paid that is well satisfied,
And I, delivering you, am satisfied,
And therein do account myself well paid;
My mind was never yet more mercenary.
I pray you know me when we meet again;   415
I wish you well, and so I take my leave.

205

417 *of force . . . further:* I am compelled to try again to persuade you.
423 *for your love:* as a token of your friendship.
433 *for this:* as for this particular (ring).
434 *liberal in offers:* very free with promises.

Questions

1 Why is Portia so keen to have the ring?
2 Do you think she has planned to do this?
3 How would you prepare the staging of this scene to contrast with all the other glimpses of Venice so far?

BASSANIO

    Dear sir, of force I must attempt you further;
    Take some remembrance of us as a tribute,
    Not as a fee. Grant me two things, I pray you:
    Not to deny me, and to pardon me.   420

PORTIA

    You press me far, and therefore I will yield.
    Give me your gloves; I'll wear them for your sake;
    And, for your love, I'll take this ring from you.
    Do not draw back your hand; I'll take no more,
    And you in love shall not deny me this!   425

BASSANIO

    This ring, good sir? Alas, it is a trifle;
    I will not shame myself to give you this!

PORTIA

    I will have nothing else but only this,
    And now methinks I have a mind to it!

BASSANIO

    There's more depends on this than on the value.   430
    The dearest ring in Venice will I give you,
    And find it out by proclamation,
    Only for this I pray you pardon me!

PORTIA

    I see, sir, you are liberal in offers;
    You taught me first to beg, and now methinks   435
    You teach me how a beggar should be answered.

BASSANIO

    Good sir, this ring was given me by my wife,
    And when she put it on, she made me vow
    That I should neither sell, nor give, nor lose it.

443   *hold . . . ever:* remain angry with you.
446–7 *Let his . . . commandement:* let his own merit and the affection you have
       for me outweigh your wife's instruction.

Questions

1 How does Bassanio attempt to avoid giving Balthazar (Portia) the
  ring without offending him?
2 Why does he give in eventually?
3 *Fly* (line 453). What feelings does Bassanio express in choosing this
  word?
4 Why is it dramatically effective to end this long scene by introducing the business of the ring rather than ending Scene 1 with
  Shylock's exit?

PORTIA

    That 'scuse serves many men to save their gifts,   440
    And if your wife be not a mad woman,
    And know how well I have deserved this ring,
    She would not hold out enemy for ever
    For giving it to me. Well, peace be with you!

                    Exeunt PORTIA *and* NERISSA

ANTONIO

    My Lord Bassanio, let him have the ring;   445
    Let his deservings and my love withal
    Be valued 'gainst your wife's commandement.

BASSANIO

    Go, Gratiano, run and overtake him,
    Give him the ring, and bring him if thou canst
    Unto Antonio's house. Away, make haste.   450

                    Exit GRATIANO

    Come, you and I will thither presently,
    And in the morning early will we both
    Fly toward Belmont. – Come, Antonio.

                    Exeunt

Scene two

Venice. A street.

Enter PORTIA *and* NERISSA.

PORTIA

    Inquire the Jew's house out; give him this deed,
    And let him sign it. We'll away to-night,
    And be a day before our husbands home.
    This deed will be well welcome to Lorenzo!

6   *upon more advice:* on further consideration.
15 *I warrant:* I'm sure.
    old swearing: any amount of swearing.
17 *outface:* boldly confront them with the facts.

Question

What is the function of this short scene?

Enter GRATIANO.

GRATIANO

Fair sir, you are well o'erta'en: 5
My Lord Bassanio, upon more advice
Hath sent you here this ring, and doth entreat
Your company at dinner.

PORTIA

                        That cannot be;
His ring I do accept most thankfully,
And so I pray you tell him. Furthermore,   10
I pray you show my youth old Shylock's house.

GRATIANO

That will I do.

NERISSA

                Sir, I would speak with you.
(*Aside to* PORTIA) I'll see if I can get my husband's
    ring,
Which I did make him swear to keep for ever.

PORTIA

Thou may'st, I warrant. We shall have old
    swearing   15
That they did give the rings away to men;
But we'll outface them, and outswear them too.
Away, make haste! Thou know'st where I will tarry.

NERISSA

Come, good sir, will you show me to this house?

                                            Exeunt

1   *In such a night:* The beauty of the night puts the newlyweds into a romantic mood in which they recall famous lovers.

4   *Troilus:* one of the sons of King Priam of Troy whose beloved, Cressida, proved unfaithful to him when she was sent as a hostage to the Greeks. Shakespeare uses this story for his play *Troilus and Cressida*.

7   *Thisbe:* Thisbe, coming to meet her lover Pyramus, was frightened by a lion with bloodstained jaws and ran away. Shakespeare gave a humorous version of this story in the play which Bottom and his companions put on at the end of *A Midsummer Night's Dream*.
    o'ertrip the dew: tiptoe across the grass.

10 *Dido:* a queen of Carthage who was deserted by the Roman hero Aeneas after a brief love affair. A branch of willow was a symbol of forsaken love.

11 *waft:* wave.

13 *Medea:* Medea stole her father's treasure and ran away with her lover, Jason, whom she helped obtain the golden fleece. She made a medicine of magic herbs to restore Jason's father, Aeson, to health. Later Jason abandoned Medea.

15 *steal:* Lorenzo puns on this word as well as on *love* (which also means 'lover') in the next line.

Question

Why does the mention of Medea remind Lorenzo of Jessica?

Act Five

Scene one

Belmont. A green place in front of Portia's house. Night-time.

Enter LORENZO *and* JESSICA.

LORENZO
The moon shines bright. In such a night as this,
When the sweet wind did gently kiss the trees,
And they did make no noise, in such a night
Troilus methinks mounted the Trojan walls,
And sighed his soul toward the Grecian tents   5
Where Cressid lay that night.

JESSICA
                In such a night
Did Thisbe fearfully o'ertrip the dew,
And saw the lion's shadow ere himself,
And ran dismayed away.

LORENZO
              In such a night
Stood Dido with a willow in her hand   10
Upon the wild sea banks, and waft her love
To come again to Carthage.

JESSICA
              In such a night
Medea gathered the enchanted herbs
That did renew old Æson.

LORENZO
              In such a night
Did Jessica steal from the wealthy Jew,   15

213

19 *stealing:* with a pun on 'steeling' – giving firmness to.
23 *out-night:* go on giving examples of lovers' exploits 'in such a night'.
   did nobody come: if no one interrupted us.
24 *footing:* footsteps.
31 *holy crosses:* wayside crosses where travellers paused to pray and make offerings.

Question

All the examples of famous love affairs given here end in misfortune. They were well known to most of the Elizabethan audience so that Shakespeare needs only to give a bare reference to each one.

How would you describe the tone of this series of exchanges between Lorenzo and Jessica? Why are there so many repetitions of the phrase *In such a night*?

And with an unthrift love did run from Venice
As far as Belmont.

JESSICA

          In such a night
Did young Lorenzo swear he loved her well,
Stealing her soul with many vows of faith,
And ne'er a true one.

LORENZO

              In such a night   20
Did pretty Jessica, like a little shrew,
Slander her love, and he forgave it her.

JESSICA

I would out-night you did nobody come:
But hark, I hear the footing of a man.

Enter STEPHANO.

LORENZO

Who comes so fast in silence of the night?   25

STEPHANO

A friend!

LORENZO

A friend! what friend? your name, I pray you,
   friend?

STEPHANO

Stephano is my name, and I bring word
My mistress will before the break of day
Be here at Belmont. She doth stray about   30
By holy crosses, where she kneels and prays
For happy wedlock hours.

LORENZO

              Who comes with her?

33   *a holy hermit:* When she set out for Venice, Portia said she was going into a monastery (Act 3, Scene 4, lines 27–32).

39   *Sola:* the sound of a messenger's horn, initiated by Launcelot.

43   *Leave hollowing:* Stop calling out!

46   *a post:* a messenger.

47   *horn:* (1) messenger's horn (2) a horn of plenty or cornucopia.

49   *expect:* wait for.

STEPHANO

None but a holy hermit and her maid.
I pray you, is my master yet returned?

LORENZO

He is not, nor we have not heard from him. –   35
But go we in, I pray thee, Jessica,
And ceremoniously let us prepare
Some welcome for the mistress of the house.

Enter LAUNCELOT.

LAUNCELOT

Sola, sola, wo ha, ho! sola, sola!

LORENZO

Who calls?   40

LAUNCELOT

Sola! did you see Master Lorenzo? Master Lorenzo,
sola, sola!

LORENZO

Leave hollowing man; here!

LAUNCELOT

Sola! where, where?

LORENZO

Here!   45

LAUNCELOT

Tell him there's a post come from my master, with
his horn full of good news; my master will be here
ere morning.

Exit

LORENZO

Sweet soul, let's in, and there expect their coming.

217

51–2 *signify . . . house:* take the news to those inside.

53 *your music:* i.e. the household musicians, such as belonged to many wealthy households.

57 *Become . . . harmony:* are fitting for the notes (*touches*) of sweet music.

59 *patens:* metal dishes. The *floor of heaven* to which Lorenzo points would be the underside of the stage roof which would have been painted to look like the sky, with stars in it.

60 *orb:* heavenly body.

62 *still quiring:* always singing. It was believed that heavenly bodies in their motion made a music which was too fine to be heard by mortal ears. Shakespeare often uses music as a symbol for harmony: social, political and spiritual.

64 *muddy vesture of decay:* soiled garment subject to corruption, i.e. the body.

66 *Diana:* the moon goddess.

67 *touches:* fingered notes. The musicians were probably on the upper stage and played violas.

70 *your spirits are attentive:* your mind is responsive.

72 *unhandled:* untrained, not broken in.

73 *Fetching mad bounds:* jumping about wildly.

74 *Which . . . blood:* which is natural in their youthful state.

Questions

1 What is the dramatic function of this interlude between the two lovers?

2 Lines 54–65. What is the importance of Lorenzo's beautiful speech to the emotional atmosphere of the play at this point?

And yet no matter; why should we go in?   50
My friend Stephano, signify, I pray you,
Within the house, your mistress is at hand,
And bring your music forth into the air.

Exit STEPHANO

How sweet the moonlight sleeps upon this bank!
Here will we sit, and let the sounds of music   55
Creep in our ears; soft stillness and the night
Become the touches of sweet harmony.
Sit, Jessica. Look how the floor of heaven
Is thick inlaid with patens of bright gold;
There's not the smallest orb which thou behold'st 60
But in his motion like an angel sings,
Still quiring to the young-eyed cherubins;
Such harmony is in immortal souls,
But whilst this muddy vesture of decay
Doth grossly close it in, we cannot hear it.   65

Enter MUSICIANS.

Come, ho! and wake Diana with a hymn!
With sweetest touches pierce your mistress' ear,
And draw her home with music.

Music

JESSICA
    I am never merry when I hear sweet music.

LORENZO
    The reason is your spirits are attentive;   70
For do but note a wild and wanton herd
Or race of youthful and unhandled colts
Fetching mad bounds, bellowing and neighing loud,
Which is the hot condition of their blood.

75   *perchance:* by chance.
77   *make a mutual stand:* all stop together.
79–80   *the poet ... floods:* Ovid, a Latin poet from whom Shakespeare borrowed much material, tells the legend of how Orpheus learned to play so skilfully on a lyre given to him by Apollo, the god of music, that beasts and even trees and rocks followed him.
81   *stockish:* lumpish, insensitive.
85   *treasons, stratagems and spoils:* treachery, plotting and plundering.
87   *affections:* emotions.
     Erebus: a part of the underworld in Greek mythology, a dark and dismal place.
97   *main of waters:* sea.

Questions

1 What qualities of Lorenzo do his speeches in lines 54–65 and lines 70–88 bring out?
2 How do these speeches enable us to understand why Jessica should dare to leave her father and her community for him?

If they but hear perchance a trumpet sound,   75
Or any air of music touch their ears,
You shall perceive them make a mutual stand,
Their savage eyes turned to a modest gaze
By the sweet power of music. Therefore the poet
Did feign that Orpheus drew trees, stones, and
    floods,   80
Since naught so stockish, hard, and full of rage,
But music for the time doth change his nature.
The man that hath no music in himself,
Nor is not moved with concord of sweet sounds,
Is fit for treasons, stratagems, and spoils;   85
The motions of his spirit are dull as night,
And his affections dark as Erebus;
Let no such man be trusted. – Mark the music.

Enter PORTIA *and* NERISSA, *at a distance from the others.*

PORTIA
That light we see is burning in my hall.
How far that little candle throws his beams!   90
So shines a good deed in a naughty world.

NERISSA
When the moon shone, we did not see the candle.

PORTIA
So doth the greater glory dim the less;
A substitute shines brightly as a king
Until a king be by, and then his state   95
Empties itself, as doth an inland brook
Into the main of waters. – Music! hark!

NERISSA
It is your music, madam, of the house.

221

99   *Nothing . . . respect:* nothing is good except by comparison with something else.

101   *Silence . . . on it:* the silence of the night makes the music sound sweeter than it does in the daytime.

103   *attended:* listened to.

107   *by season seasoned:* appreciated because they take place at the appropriate time.

109   *Endymion:* In Greek legend, the moon goddess fell in love with the beautiful youth, Endymion, and put him into an eternal sleep so that she would forever lie beside him.

115   *Which . . . our words:* we hope our husband's fortunes have benefitted by our words.

Questions

1 How does the conversation between Portia and Nerissa affect the atmosphere of the scene?

2 Reflecting on all their previous conversations, why should we conclude that Nerissa's company is so important to Portia, more important than is usual between a lady and her maid? What qualities in Nerissa does this closeness suggest?

3 Lines 114–15. What is the irony in these lines?

PORTIA

> Nothing is good, I see, without respect;
> Methinks it sounds much sweeter than by day.　　100

NERISSA

> Silence bestows that virtue on it, madam.

PORTIA

> The crow doth sing as sweetly as the lark
> When neither is attended; and I think
> The nightingale, if she should sing by day,
> When every goose is cackling, would be thought　　105
> No better a musician than the wren!
> How many things by season seasoned are
> To their right praise, and true perfection!
> Peace! – how the moon sleeps with Endymion,
> And would not be awaked!

Music ceases.

LORENZO

> 　　　　　　　　　That is the voice,　　110
> Or I am much deceived, of Portia.

PORTIA

> He knows me as the blind man knows the cuckoo –
> By the bad voice!

LORENZO

> 　　　　　Dear lady, welcome home!

PORTIA

> We have been praying for our husbands' welfare,
> Which speed, we hope, the better for our words.　　115
> Are they returned?

LORENZO

> 　　　　Madam, they are not yet;

117 *before:* in advance.

119–120 *they take . . . hence:* they make no mention of our absence.

127–8 *We should . . . the sun:* if you (Portia) walked at night, we should have daylight at the same time as the other side of the earth (because of your radiance).

129 *light:* with a pun on *light* as loose in morals.

132 *God sort all:* dispose of all, sort it all out.

135 *bound:* the word 'bound' reminds us of the seriousness of Antonio's previous 'bond'. Bassanio means that he owes Antonio everything.

Questions

1 How do you account for the number of references to light?

2 Lines 129–30. What does Portia's response to Bassanio's extravagant compliment add to our knowledge of her character and her sense of humour?

But there is come a messenger before
To signify their coming.

PORTIA

                Go in, Nerissa.
Give order to my servants that they take
No note at all of our being absent hence;   120
Nor you, Lorenzo; Jessica, nor you.

A tucket sounds.

LORENZO

Your husband is at hand; I hear his trumpet;
We are no tell-tales, madam; fear you not.

PORTIA

This night methinks is but the daylight sick;
It looks a little paler – 't is a day   125
Such as the day is when the sun is hid.

Enter BASSANIO, ANTONIO, GRATIANO, *and their followers.*

BASSANIO

We should hold day with the Antipodes,
If you would walk in absence of the sun.

PORTIA

Let me *give* light, but let me not *be* light,
For a light wife doth make a heavy husband,   130
And never be Bassanio so for me. –
But God sort all! You are welcome home, my
    lord.

BASSANIO

I thank you, madam. Give welcome to my friend;
This is the man, this is Antonio,
To whom I am so infinitely bound.   135

136   *in all sense:* in all respects.

      bound: a joking reference to all Antonio's bonds, of love, the bond to Shylock, and perhaps also the chains in which he was bound as a prisoner.

138   *acquitted of:* Antonio means that Bassanio has discharged or cleared any moral debt he was under just as he (Antonio) has been acquitted, i.e. set free of the crime he was charged with.

140   *It:* i.e. the fact that he is welcome.

141   *I scant this breathing courtesy:* I'll cut short these polite words.

144   *gelt:* gelded, castrated.

148   *posy:* motto engraved inside a ring.

149   *cutler's poetry:* poetry written by the knife-maker, i.e. doggerel or verse of low quality.

155–6   *Though not . . . respective:* even if you had no regard for me, you should have respected your own emphatic promises.

PORTIA
You should in all sense be much bound to him,
For, as I hear, he was much bound for you.

ANTONIO
No more than I am well acquitted of.

PORTIA
(*To* ANTONIO) Sir, you are very welcome to our
house.
It must appear in other ways than words;   140
Therefore I scant this breathing courtesy.

GRATIANO
(*To* NERISSA) By yonder moon I swear you do me
wrong;
In faith I gave it to the judge's clerk
Would he were gelt that had it for my part,
Since you do take it, love, so much at heart.   145

PORTIA
A quarrel, ho, already! What's the matter?

GRATIANO
About a hoop of gold, a paltry ring
That she did give me, whose posy was
For all the world like cutler's poetry
Upon a knife: "Love me, and leave me not."   150

NERISSA
What talk you of the posy or the value?
You swore to me when I did give it you
That you would wear it till your hour of death,
And that it should lie with you in your grave.
Though not for me, yet for your vehement oaths   155
You should have been respective and have kept it.

227

162   *scrubbèd:* stunted in his growth.
164   *prating:* nagging.
173–4   *for the wealth . . . masters:* for all the wealth in the world.

Questions

1 How does Bassanio's account of Gratiano in Act 2, Scene 2, lines 178–82 apply to his behaviour at this point?
2 What is the dramatic effect of Nerissa's quarrel with Gratiano about her ring?

Gave it a judge's clerk! no, God's my judge,
The clerk will ne'er wear hair on's face that had it.

GRATIANO

He will, and if he live to be a man.

NERISSA

Ay, if a woman live to be a man.   160

GRATIANO

Now, by this hand, I gave it to a youth,
A kind of boy, a little scrubbèd boy,
No higher than thyself, the judge's clerk,
A prating boy that begged it as a fee.
I could not for my heart deny it him.   165

PORTIA

You were to blame, I must be plain with you,
To part so slightly with your wife's first gift,
A thing stuck on with oaths upon your finger,
And so riveted with faith unto your flesh.
I gave my love a ring, and made him swear   170
Never to part with it, and here he stands:
I dare be sworn for him he would not leave it,
Nor pluck it from his finger, for the wealth
That the world masters. Now, in faith, Gratiano,
You give your wife too unkind a cause of grief;   175
An't were to me I should be mad at it.

BASSANIO (Aside)

Why, I were best to cut my left hand off,
And swear I lost the ring defending it.

GRATIANO

My Lord Bassanio gave his ring away
Unto the judge that begged it, and indeed   180
Deserved it too; and then the boy, his clerk,

229

189   *void:* empty.
195   *conceive:* understand fully. Bassanio attempts to impress upon Portia the importance of the circumstances referred to. Portia mocks him by parodying his own rhythms in her reply.
198   *abate:* reduce, moderate.
201   *contain:* keep.
203–6   *What man . . . ceremony?* What man would be so unreasonable, so insensitive as to insist on your giving up what you should have kept as a symbol of faith, if you had cared enough to defend it with any real enthusiasm?

Questions

1 Lines 190–3. Why are Portia and Nerissa quite safe in making these oaths about their rings?

2 What is our impression of Bassanio when he attempts to excuse himself to Portia?

3 Lines 199–202. What truth is there in Portia's rejoinder to Bassanio's attempts to soothe her?

That took some pains in writing, he begged mine,
And neither man nor master would take aught
But the two rings.

PORTIA

       What ring gave you, my lord?
Not that, I hope, which you received of me.   185

BASSANIO

If I could add a lie unto a fault,
I would deny it; but you see my finger
Hath not the ring upon it; it is gone.

PORTIA

Even so void is your false heart of truth.
By heaven I will ne'er come in your bed   190
Until I see the ring!

NERISSA

(*To* GRATIANO)   Nor I in yours
Till I again see mine!

BASSANIO

       Sweet Portia,
If you did know to whom I gave the ring,
If you did know for whom I gave the ring,
And would conceive for what I gave the ring,   195
And how unwillingly I left the ring,
When nought would be accepted but the ring,
You would abate the strength of your displeasure.

PORTIA

If you had known the virtue of the ring,
Or half her worthiness that gave the ring,   200
Or your own honour to contain the ring,
You would not then have parted with the ring.
What man is there so much unreasonable,

210 *a civil doctor:* doctor of civil law (with a pun on *civil* – well-mannered).
211 *Which:* who.
213 *suffered:* allowed.
214 *held up:* defended.
217 *I was . . . courtesy:* I was overwhelmed with shame and the demands of courteous behaviour.
219 *besmear:* stain.
220 *candles of the night:* stars.
226 *liberal:* (1) overgenerous (2) loose in morals.
229 *know:* with a play in the biblical sense, meaning 'to have sexual intercourse'.
230 *Lie not . . . home:* do not spend even one night away from home.
    Argus: In Greek legend, a monster with a hundred eyes, some of which were always open.
232 *which is yet mine own:* a mocking reference to Bassanio who has lost his honour by breaking his word, and a reminder of her own virgin state in spite of her marriage to Bassanio.

Questions

1 What is the dramatic irony in this dialogue?
2 Do you find anything distasteful in Portia's speech to Bassanio? How should it be played?

If you had pleased to have defended it
With any terms of zeal, wanted the modesty   205
To urge the thing held as a ceremony?
Nerissa teaches me what to believe:
I'll die for 't, but some woman had the ring!

BASSANIO

No, by my honour, madam, by my soul,
No woman had it, but a civil doctor,   210
Which did refuse three thousand ducats of me,
And begged the ring; the which I did deny him,
And suffered him to go displeased away,
Even he that had held up the very life
Of my dear friend. What should I say, sweet lady? 215
I was enforced to send it after him;
I was beset with shame and courtesy;
My honour would not let ingratitude
So much besmear it. Pardon me, good lady,
For by these blessèd candles of the night,   220
Had you been there, I think you would have
    begged
The ring of me to give the worthy doctor.

PORTIA

Let not that doctor e'er come near my house.
Since he hath got the jewel that I loved,
And that which you did swear to keep for me,   225
I will become as liberal as you;
I'll not deny him anything I have,
No, not my body, nor my husband's bed;
Know him I shall, I am well sure of it.
Lie not a night from home. Watch me like Argus;   230
If you do not, if I be left alone,
Now by mine honour, which is yet mine own,
I'll have that doctor for my bedfellow.

234 *be well advised:* take good care.
237 *I'll mar . . . pen:* a bawdy joke – 'I'll castrate him' with a pun on *pen*, the mark of a clerk's profession.
240 *forgive . . . wrong:* pardon me for doing this wrong which I was forced to do.
243 *Mark you but that:* just listen to him.
245 *double:* with a pun on 'two-faced' (false).
246 *an oath of credit:* a believable oath.
251 *quite miscarried:* gone wrong entirely, (my body) would have been lost.

Question

Describe and account for the different responses of Bassanio and Gratiano at this point.

NERISSA

    And I his clerk; therefore be well advised

    How you do leave me to mine own protection.   235

GRATIANO

    Well, do you so; let not me take him then,

    For if I do, I'll mar the young clerk's pen.

ANTONIO

    I am th' unhappy subject of these quarrels.

PORTIA

    Sir, grieve not you; you are welcome notwithstand-

       ing.

BASSANIO

    Portia, forgive me this enforcèd wrong,   240

    And, in the hearing of these many friends,

    I swear to thee, even by thine own fair eyes,

    Wherein I see myself –

PORTIA

                   Mark you but that

    In both my eyes he doubly sees himself;

    In each eye one; swear by your double self,   245

    And there's an oath of credit.

BASSANIO

                 Nay, but hear me.

    Pardon this fault, and by my soul I swear

    I never more will break an oath with thee.

ANTONIO

    I once did lend my body for his wealth

    Which, but for him that had your husband's

       ring,   250

    Had quite miscarried. I dare be bound again,

253   *advisedly:* knowingly.

262   *in lieu of this:* in return for this (ring).

263-4 *this is like ... enough:* In summer, when it is dry, roads needed no mending. In winter time, many roads in Elizabethan England were little better than muddy ditches.

265   *What ... deserved it?:* Gratiano jokingly implies that only men who have been unfaithful to their wives deserve to have wives who are unfaithful to them.

266   *grossly:* coarsely.

Questions

1 What are our feelings towards Antonio during this scene and how does his promise (lines 251–3) affect them?

2 Why do you think Portia feels the joke has gone far enough and tells Bassanio and Gratiano the plain truth?

236

My soul upon the forfeit, that your lord
Will never more break faith advisedly.

PORTIA
Then you shall be his surety. Give him this,
And bid him keep it better than the other.   255

She gives ANTONIO *a ring.*

ANTONIO
Here, Lord Bassanio, swear to keep this ring.

BASSANIO
By heaven it is the same I gave the doctor!

PORTIA
I had it of him; pardon me, Bassanio,
For by this ring the doctor lay with me.

NERISSA
And pardon me, my gentle Gratiano,   260
For that same scrubbèd boy, the doctor's clerk,
In lieu of this, last night did lie with me.

GRATIANO
Why this is like the mending of highways
In summer, where the ways are fair enough!
What, are we cuckolds ere we have deserved it?   265

PORTIA
Speak not so grossly. You are all amazed;
Here is a letter; read it at your leisure;
It comes from Padua, from Bellario.
There you shall find that Portia was the doctor,
Nerissa there her clerk. Lorenzo here   270
Shall witness I set forth as soon as you,
And even but now returned; I have not yet
Entered my house. Antonio, you are welcome,

275 *soon:* now.
277 *suddenly:* unexpectedly.
279 *chancèd on:* came across.
286 *living:* means of livelihood.
288 *Are safely . . . road:* are safely anchored.

And I have better news in store for you
Than you expect. Unseal this letter soon;   275
There you shall find three of your argosies
Are richly come to harbour suddenly.
You shall not know by what strange accident
I chancèd on this letter.

ANTONIO

I am dumb!

BASSANIO

Were you the doctor, and I knew you not?   280

GRATIANO

Were you the clerk that is to make me cuckold?

NERISSA

Ay, but the clerk that never means to do it,
Unless he live until he be a man.

BASSANIO

Sweet doctor, you shall be my bedfellow;
When I am absent then lie with my wife.   285

ANTONIO

Sweet lady, you have given me life and living;
For here I read for certain that my ships
Are safely come to road.

PORTIA

How now, Lorenzo?
My clerk hath some good comforts too for you.

NERISSA

Ay, and I'll give them him without a fee.   290
There do I give to you and Jessica,
From the rich Jew, a special deed of gift,
After his death, of all he dies possessed of.

239

294 *manna:* heavenly food sent to the Israelites (*Exodus* 26.14–21), hence, any unexpected gift or favour.

298 *charge us . . . inter'gatories:* ask questions which we shall answer on oath (as in court). A continuance of the mild legal joking which appears earlier in Nerissa's reference to a fee (line 290).

307 *So sore:* so much.

Questions

1 Describe the *good comforts* Portia and Nerissa bring to all the others on stage with them at the end of the scene.

2 Compare the responses of Antonio and Lorenzo.

3 How would you describe the tone of Gratiano's final speech?

4 How would you arrange the characters' exit from the stage to round off the play to your own satisfaction?

LORENZO

Fair ladies, you drop manna in the way
Of starvèd people.

PORTIA

It is almost morning,   295
And yet I am sure you are not satisfied
Of these events at full. Let us go in,
And charge us there upon inter'gatories,
And we will answer all things faithfully.

GRATIANO

Let it be so; the first inter'gatory   300
That my Nerissa shall be sworn on is,
Whether till the next night she had rather stay,
Or go to bed now, being two hours to day;
But were the day come, I should wish it dark
Till I were couching with the doctor's clerk.   305
Well, while I live I'll fear no other thing
So sore as keeping safe Nerissa's ring.

Exeunt

Studying *The Merchant of Venice*

Text and performance

The earliest printed text of *The Merchant of Venice* is dated 1600 but the play was probably written between 1594 and 1598 and performed fairly frequently before it was printed. This text is called the Quarto edition (after the practice of folding up large sheets to make four leaves) and only a handful of copies remain in Britain now. The title page gives a description of the play's story-line:

> The most excellent Historie of the Merchant of
> Venice. With the extreame crueltie of Shylocke the
> Iewe towards the sayd Merchant, in cutting a iust
> pound of his flesh: and the obtayning of Portia by the
> choyse of three chests. As it hath been divers times
> acted by the Lord Chamberlaine his Seruants.
> Written by William Shakespeare.

Shakespeare's company of actors, the Lord Chamberlain's Men, later the King's Men, was the leading theatrical troupe of its day. Their first *recorded* performance of the play took place in February 1605 before King James the First who liked it so well that he called for a repeat performance a week later!

What did the printer mean by calling the play 'a most excellent Historie'? Originally, a history was a kind of writing considered to be factually true. Later, the term came to be used of narratives which though not actually true expressed *moral* truths, like parables in the Bible.

An 'excellent Historie' then, would be a play which dealt with real or invented events in such a way that its moral lessons were effectively brought home to the audience. *The Merchant of Venice*, therefore, was regarded as an excellent means of teaching those who watched it something about the right ways and the wrong ways to behave towards their fellow men.

Shakespeare did not invent the two main strands of the plot, the extreme cruelty of Shylock the Jew, and the winning of Portia, mentioned in the description above. A collection of Italian stories published in England in 1580 contained a story called *Il Pecorone* ('Simpleton') which told how a young Venetian nobleman called Giannetto borrowed all his godfather's money to finance voyages meant to make his fortune. Giannetto becomes infatuated by the mysterious Lady of Belmont, a beautiful young widow, who tricks him out of his ships as he attempts to win her as his bride.

His loving godfather has contracted himself to a Jewish money-lender to pay a pound of his flesh if he cannot repay by an agreed date the money he has borrowed to help Gian-netto. When the money is overdue, the Jew demands his pound of flesh. The Lady of Belmont, now Giannetto's wife, disguises herself as a lawyer and goes to Venice where she establishes that the Jew cannot shed a drop of blood in taking his pound of flesh, saves the godfather, and tricks her husband out of the ring she has given him earlier. The story ends happily with Giannetto, his godfather, and the Lady celebrating the fortunate outcome of all their schemes in Belmont.

The Casket story comes from an old tale translated from Latin and popular in Britain from Medieval times. The hero in the original, the *source* story, proves his worth by choosing the least attractive casket, and ignoring those which attract the greedy and the vain.

In Shakespeare's play, Bassanio's moral worth, and Portia's obedience to her father's will, are the dramatist's own invention, as is the personality of Shylock, who is very different from the anonymous Jew of the Italian story.

Giving topical relevance to an old story or a familiar theme was one of Shakespeare's many talents. His originality consists in the way he blended elements from sources of proven narra-tive interest to suit his own dramatic purposes. But why should

Shakespeare have called up from his memory a tale about a merchant and a Jew? In his introductory essay, David Suchet has explained why a play on such a subject might have appealed to the dramatist at this particular period. Marlowe's play, *The Jew of Malta*, was performed fifteen times by another troupe, from the time of the arrest of Roderigo Lopez until the end of the year in which he was hanged for treason. In 1596, the probable year of the writing of *The Merchant of Venice*, Marlowe's play was performed eight times between 9 January and 23 June. In the previous year, anti-alien riots had flared up in London during a period of shortage of food caused by bad harvests.

Clearly, the success of a rival's play, performed by a rival theatrical company, plus the anxiety among Londoners about foreigners who had settled in England must have influenced Shakespeare in his choice of a play which would make his company successful and solvent.

Shakespeare's society: commercial enterprise and usury

Writers are motivated by many different factors. Analysing and accounting for these factors is the business of scholars who research the period in which their chosen writer lived. Their findings are often quite fascinating to read for the understanding they give us of the period in which the writer was working. Now, the writer is not an impartial observer of his own time and the political and economic implications of his own society, as an historian should be. Those aspects which he selects to write about must mesh with his own deepest interests and the drives which subconsciously compel him to write plays, poetry, and books instead of using his energies, his intelligence, and his imagination in some different field of enterprise. An artist can never be finally *explained* by scholarship and criticism. Nevertheless, it is interesting to examine *The Merchant of Venice* in the light of what we know about the Elizabethan period.

244

A new class

This is a fascinating play, not least because of the way it presents the emergence of a social class whose activities are at least as interesting as those of the nobility upon whom most stories and plays had been focused. A new commercial class, the merchant adventurers, entrepreneurs as we could call them now, and a new economy based upon money rather than land were rapidly coming into being, stimulated by the expansion of foreign trade among other things. Opening up the globe to trade took enormous courage and daring, dependent as it was upon personal risk in the small and vulnerable ships which had to encounter not only the elements but also the ships of their enemies on the high seas. The excellence of British wool enabled British merchants to dominate the markets in Europe, but it was the seamanship and adventurousness of sailors like Sir Francis Drake which enabled the British to outstrip their European rivals for world markets. (Drake was regularly described as 'the English pirate' by the German merchants in their news-sheets which circulated throughout Europe.)

This was an era of risk taking: it saw the emergence of a class of men anxious to make their fortunes, and to establish their status, in a society which had been dominated by the land-based rule of the aristocrats with their inherited wealth. Money was essential to the new economy. A commercial state depends upon the borrowing and repayment of money, its buying and selling in fact, to carry out its reason for existence – the encouragement of trade that makes men first rich, then powerful.

The enmity that exists between Antonio the merchant, and Shylock the Jewish money-lender exists before *The Merchant of Venice* begins. It is grounded in *mutual* contempt.

On Antonio's side we have contempt for usury and usurers, the money-lenders who charge interest on their loans. On Shylock's, there is contempt for the 'low simplicity' which will not allow Antonio to recognize the fact that money itself is a commodity in a commercial society which exists by buying goods like spices and silks cheaply at source, and selling them at a profit elsewhere. The risks taken by the merchant in the transportation of goods can be matched, in Shylock's view, by the risk taken by the financier whose money – *his* only 'commodity' – he puts in hazard. His share of the gains is the interest he charges in order that other men can pursue their commercial ventures.

Antonio is old fashioned, a simpleton, seen from Shylock's perspective. Shylock has travelled, lives as an alien in Venice, has bought jewellery in Frankfurt. He knows the world. Moral disapproval of charging interest is appropriate only to a society based on the ownership of land, where borrowing money would be exceptional – during a bad harvest or a family disaster, for example. Borrowing money among merchant adventurers, however, is a means of financing profit-making by men daring, enterprising and ruthless enough to turn pirate should the need arise.

Bassanio is, after all, a fortune-hunter as well as a prospective husband, as the image of the arrow which he uses (Act 1, Scene 1, lines 140–52) clearly asserts. Gratiano underlines the 'commercial' nature of their enterprise in his greeting to Salerio after Portia has been won:

> How doth that royal merchant good Antonio?
> I know he will be glad of success;
> We are the Jasons, we have won the fleece.

> (Act 3, Scene 2, lines 238–40)

The money borrowed from Shylock has thus been used in a successful gamble, not to supply a real need.

From Shylock's view-point, to charge interest is to attempt to profit from a commercial transaction like any other. And Portia's question as she enters the court room can be seen as ironically apt:

> Which is the merchant here? and which the Jew?

246

That Shylock takes a realistic view of such transactions is evident from the tone and language he uses to justify his actions. The lengthy allusion from the Bible story of Jacob is intended to show that he allies himself with the fathers of his nation who used the opportunity offered by the society in which they found themselves to 'thrive' by enterprise and initiative. This offends the Christians yet they, too, feel the need to make their enterprise respectable by alluding to themselves as 'Jasons', invoking the Greek heroes' mythical quest to glamourize a spot of fortune-hunting!

To Shylock, money is 'the prop that doth sustain my house' but then his cargoes are 'life and living' to Antonio. Shylock cannot therefore understand why Antonio should show him such contempt when he needs what only Shylock and his like can provide. He cannot believe that a *merchant* could be so naive. As well as the desire to score points, there is also genuine incredulity in his famous speech in Act 1, Scene 2 when he asks 'Is it possible a cur can lend three thousand ducats?'

Both are incapable of understanding the other's point of view and the basis of their contempt is prejudice. Each uses religion as a means to explain to himself the other's motivtion. To Antonio, Shylock's 'Jewish heart' accounts for his lack of mercy in business dealings. While to Shylock, Antonio's reason for spitting on him is that Antonio is a Christian who hates Shylock's 'sacred nation'.

Had Antonio not existed, Shylock would have made a million. Had Shylock not existed, Bassanio could not have assembled the social trappings of servants, fine liveries and presents which made him a credible suitor for an heiress.

Accustomed as we are now to banks, building societies and finance companies, we may find it difficult to imagine a time when a loan desperately needed could come only from a wealthy friend or from a money-lender whose financial activities were regarded as disreputable and degrading. To understand a little better the society within which the play was written we need to consider both the position of Jews in

247

European society and the significance of Venice as the play's main location.

Christians and Jews

Most people who saw Marlowe's *The Jew of Malta* and Shakespeare's *The Merchant of Venice* had little firsthand knowledge of Jews. Very few Jewish people lived in England and those who did had to modify their religious practices. In England, prejudice against Jews never reached the heights that it did in Catholic countries where the hated and hateful Inquisition was a powerful force.

The Inquisition was an ecclesiastical tribunal organized in the thirteenth century by Pope Innocent III to suppress heresy and punish heretics. For centuries it hounded and persecuted those who did not conform to standard Catholic practice of the Christian religion, using torture to obtain confessions, and allowing to be burned people like St Joan of Arc, who were suspected of putting their own consciences above the Church's teachings. In Catholic countries, non-Catholics were not permitted to practise their religions. In some parts of Italy, Jews were compelled to wear special clothes which marked them as outsiders – at a time when clothes were an important sign of one's place in the social order. A Jew's cloak, cap, or badge, indicated that he was an alien who did not belong within that order. In Venice, in the Ghetto, a part of the city reserved exclusively for Jews, their homes and families were physically separated from those who were citizens by rights, though they could engage in business on the Rialto.

In Spain, their situation was worse. If they practised their religion they were burned. If they recanted and became Christians, they served a period of time in the galleys, and their goods were confiscated.

England was a Protestant country whose great enemy was Catholic Spain. One of the crowning glories of Elizabeth's reign was the defeat of the Spanish Armada and the 'wealthy

Andrew' (Act 1, Scene 1, lines 25–9) of the play is probably a reference to the 'San Andrea', the Spanish Vice-Admiral's ship and the pride of the fleet, which Drake captured and gave to the Queen's navy where it tended to run aground regularly, much to the annoyance of the Earl of Essex!

Judged by these standards of cruelty, the treatment of Shylock in the play may be called lenient. King James probably thoroughly approved of Shylock's forced conversion, knowing what would have become of him in Catholic Europe. Nevertheless, the trial which began as Antonio's ends ironically as Shylock's. In a slave-owning society what could a Jew expect?

To ordinary English people, Jews were vaguely sinister characters suspected of deeprooted hatred of Christ, child murder, poisoning of public wells, and other dark deeds. Outside London, most English people had never seen a foreigner. Only the educated, the influential, and the wealthy travelled widely, on diplomatic missions, within the intellectual community, or for purposes of war and trade. They would have been a small minority in the audience. In Shakespeare's *Henry V*, even the Irish, the Scots, and the Welsh among Henry's soldiers are treated as rather eccentric outsiders.

Shakespeare seems to have found much personal amusement at his countrymen's tendency to regard foreigners as caricatures of real people. The kind of national stereotypes created by ignorance, rumour and prejudice are paraded before us by Portia in Act 1, Scene 2. The tendency to despise foreigners seems as firmly entrenched in Shakespeare's England as it is today. But we should note that Shakespeare includes the English Lord among those who are made to look ridiculous by the civilized standards of Belmont.

Only the Jew, the Moor, and the Spaniard appear in person, to be judged by others and ourselves. And only the Jew among these engages Shakespeare's major interest in the play. Shakespeare seems to have understood very clearly the reasons for their importance at this period. Among all those who lent money to the great and powerful, Jews stood out as a *racial* group celebrated for their business ability. They were also widely regarded as misers because their wealth was not displayed and was therefore considered to have been hoarded. (Whatever truth there is in this charge is easily explained when we read in contemporary documents of Jews whose wealth was stolen from them and who were reduced to slavery in the galleys by unscrupulous European rulers.)

The Jews used their skills in the lending and investment of money to finance the merchants who borrowed in the hope of a successful voyage. Some of the great European financial institutions of today stem from hard-headed 'survivors', to use David Suchet's term, like Shylock, living as outcasts in the Europe of Shakespeare's time.

Many of those in the original audience would have sided with the borrower for personal reasons, and many in the cast as well, for English noblemen and the new business men owed thousands to nameless financiers whose dealings can be discovered by researching the commercial documents of the period. But only the Jews could be easily identified, largely because they were forced to identify themselves, as outsiders in a society which called itself Christian.

Venice and Belmont

Why Venice? Venice was the location of the main source story in *Il Pecorone* but the significance of Shakespeare's retention of that city as the context for his play requires more examination. To the Elizabethan audience, Venice would have signified a number of things. Wealthy and splendid, the independent city-state was a symbol of magnificence, whose wealth came by water. Its magnificence belongs to the historical period called the Renaissance, which means the rebirth or the revival of art and literature under the influence of classical models, which began in Italy in the fourteenth century. Venice was a centre of Renaissance art, famous for the beauty of its buildings, their interior decorations, its paintings, and its music.

The Venetian Republic was secular, outside the grasp of the Inquisition, and a society of great sophistication. (Venetians invented income tax, the gambling casino, and the science of statistics, among other things.) But more importantly for our purposes, it was politically and socially unique. Dependent almost wholly on trade for its existence, it had a legal system which was designed to promote and protect commerce while the rights of the individual, including those of foreigners, were totally safeguarded. In some ways it was a model of what Britain would regard itself as being today.

Freedom of thought and of speech are important rights, especially to the dramatist. (Shakespeare's players were once charged with complicity in the rebellion of the Earl of Essex after an ill-timed performance of *Richard II*!)

Shakespeare contents himself with underlining Venice's well known legal position in Antonio's speech in Act 3, Scene 3:

The duke cannot deny the course of law;
For the commodity that strangers have
With us in Venice, if it be denied,
Will much impeach the justice of the state,
Since that the trade and profit of the city
Consisteth of all nations.

Two of Shakespeare's plays, *Othello* and *The Merchant of Venice*, are set in Venice. Othello is a Moor, a black man, and presumably a Muslim, and Shylock is a Jew. In both plays, prejudice against an alien is an important theme and it is not Christianity but the laws of the Venetian Republic which operate to safeguard the rights of outsiders, even when complaints are made against them by leading citizens of the state.

If the doings of merchants were to be considered as interesting to an audience as those of princes, then to place the play in Venice was to borrow an aura of glamour from its very name. Extravagant things were to be expected from Venetians.

Trade and profit were known to be the foundation of the

prosperity of Venice. Its legal system reflected the kind of treatment of foreigners that such a state required, whatever the private opinions and prejudice of its citizens. We note the contrast between Portia's public and her private comments on the black Prince of Morocco. Yet, whatever her opinion, she would have married him had he chosen the right casket.

A fact of which we are generally unaware today is that Venetian women were regarded as being sophisticated to the point of being licentious in Shakespeare's time. Pornographic pamphlets often had a Venetian courtesan in a starring role. Othello is led to suspect his Venetian wife Desdemona of infidelity by reminders of the reputation of her nation's women; and Shakespeare is careful in creating Portia of Belmont to invoke the name of Portia, the Roman wife of Brutus, in his *Julius Caesar*, a woman of such virtue that she committed suicide in case she might betray her husband's political intentions. Portia of Belmont's respect for the law of her country is exemplified in her stern treatment of Shylock once he had firmly rejected her pleas for mercy in favour of the impersonal and formal dealings of justice.

As an already established centre of commerce, Venice was a model for what London aspired to be. By reminding his audience of the tolerance of foreigners, the religious freedom and the penalty for prejudice which its legal system sternly enforced, Shakespeare emphasized the standards which a successful commercial nation would have to enforce upon its people.

Belmont is only a short ferry trip away from Venice and its Rialto, where the necessity of obtaining three thousand ducats can imperil a merchant's life. However, it is, in more senses than one, a different world from the turmoil and bustling activity of the Rialto. The pace of life is leisurely and unharassed for all those who live or come there, and its values are those of grace, courtesy, and generosity – at least for those within the charmed circle of Portia's friendship or affection.

The grace and charm of Belmont are attained by shutting out the sordid world of Venice with beauty, music, and moonlight. Yet these are supported by a reservoir of money greater than Shylock could count. Portia's wealth is inherited and she is the richest person in the play. Is she a retired merchant's daughter or a true aristocrat? That her relative is an academic kind of lawyer suggests that she is a member of the new middle class rather than of the nobility, though princes and dukes consider her of sufficient rank to ally themselves in marriage with her.

It would be profitless to pursue the implications of her status too far. Whatever her origins, Portia and whoever wins her as his bride have reached the secure shores of uncountable wealth where the charm of culture may be enjoyed in full with a retinue of servants, a marvellous garden, and household musicians to make moonlight evocative of legend. Yet, like the fairytale princess, Portia is condemned to her enchanted palace until Bassanio comes to rescue her, with all the verve and nerve of commercial Venice to aid him. Then, balance is achieved and Belmont is restored. Portia and her home are transformed. Once liberated by love, her fierce intelligence is set free to operate within a new arena, not previously open to her as a woman. Ironically, though, it is the carefully counted out money of Shylock the Jew which supplies the key!

Without Belmont, the aspiration and dream of those who strive for wealth, Venice is masculine, harsh, and tawdry. Without Venice, Belmont is a gilded cage in which an intelligent woman is stifled to the point of feeling that her 'little body is a weary of this great world'. Her will is curbed and her scope limited until Bassanio comes like a fairytale Prince Charming to free her. Her energy and resourcefulness are much needed in Venice, tempered with the humanity which Venice seems to lack.

Venice was called 'La Serenissima' by those who admired the city's art, its taste, and beauty. Belmont represents that aspect of Venice, and Portia its embodiment; beautiful, gracious, and courteous but with a keen wit, and a shrewd grasp of law and its practicalities concealed at the centre.

The contrasting locales of Venice and Belmont embody

much of the play's themes and meaning but they are not separate. They penetrate each other, as the theme of Shylock's cruelty, which takes hold of Bassanio's and Antonio's scheme, and the casket theme interpenetrate, to give the play its power to endure and to be relevant.

Interpretations

It is not necessary to know the social and economic background of *The Merchant of Venice* before we can enjoy the play and understand its characters. David Suchet has explained how an interest in historical context enabled him to understand how other actors had seen the role of Shylock and how he could create his own interpretation. Photographs in a later section provide us with examples of contrasting productions with different interpretations of what the play seems to signify to directors and actors. Part of our study must be to show how opportunities to do just this exist in Shakespeare's play. That is precisely why Shakespeare has engaged the interest of generations of actors, audiences, and scholars. Things are never made so cut and dried by the playwright, nor so explained away by theatre critics and academics that there isn't room for our feeling that *we* have discovered something more about the plotting or the people of the play than already exists in productions and in print.

If you attend a particularly appealing production, you may think that *this* is the way Shakespeare intended the scene to be performed, or a character to be portrayed, but much depends upon the way the stage is dressed, upon the sheer physical presence of the actors chosen, and upon the period from which the costumes are selected. Shakespeare's own stage was relatively bare, and the costumes were generally the clothes of his own day, selected according to the rank of the characters involved. It was the language of the speeches which created the world of the play as it emerged in the imagination of the playwright.

254

We can never know, though, exactly how it *sounded* since pronunciation and accent have changed since the Elizabethan period. Shakespeare's actors may have sounded more like Ulstermen than Londoners, for example. And the effect of boys acting Portia and Jessica as well as Nerissa should not be underestimated, for much of the humour of the play is lost upon us now when we see women rather thinly disguised as young men.

Despite the importance of watching the play in performance, teachers have always laid great stress upon a close study of the text itself. It is through the rather painful examination of the language that there does emerge again, in our own imaginations, the personalities of the people of the play, and a true and personal grasp of their human and understandable concerns.

What do *you* think of the characters as people, and how would *you* perform their parts in particular scenes? You must bear your own views in mind when you read someone else's comments and criticisms. No one interpretation has the authority to impose a particular reading upon you, Shakespeare's imagined audience for the play he wrote. The study questions will help you to come to your own conclusions as you wrestle with the meanings, the emerging themes, the dramatic qualities, and the subtle ironies of the play. We shall confine our further comments to a consideration of the most important characters.

Friendship, hatred, and love

The play is about the interplay of these emotions and we do not require much scholarship to respond to them. If we use these three different emotions as guidelines, we can focus our interest upon Portia, Antonio, and Shylock as the main centres of dramatic attention. How do they address us?

Initially, Shylock addresses the audience directly and confidentially, thrusting his plans upon us in an almost subversive way; but once he becomes involved in the action of the plot, he becomes engrossed with his own plight as much as with revenge and eventually his bitterness and his anger are openly addressed to the other characters and to the world at large. His hatred hardens to obsession as his sense of persecution reinforces his natural harshness.

Portia's personal side is revealed to Nerissa and thus to us. Her only soliloquy, clarifying, as soliloquies always do, what she is truly feeling, is her speech while Bassanio is choosing the casket which will unlock her prison. It is an outpouring of hope and love which contrasts with Shylock's hatred and contempt.

Interestingly, Antonio reveals little of himself except through speeches in which he *responds* to others. His letter is terse and unemotional, though vibrant with unstated or understated feeling.

Friendship: Antonio

We meet Antonio at the outset, perplexing his friends with a melancholy which he cannot or will not explain. Worries about his financial affairs are denied, and suggestions of his being in love are brushed aside as if they were somehow unseemly for a man of his age. At the end of the play he is in Belmont with the rest, but unlike them, without a partner. His mysterious references to himself, scattered throughout the play, suggest that he is as conscious of his difference from others as Shylock is, but he offers no explanation for his sense of isolation.

Unlike Portia, who plays her various roles – heiress, lover, lawyer, wife, friend – with gusto, Antonio seems disillusioned and fatalistic. Yet as a man of affairs he has been enterprising and successful, sending his argosies throughout the world, and as a citizen, he has attacked the practice of usury, helping to rescue those who have become its victims. On hearing of Bassanio's plan, he is ready to act immediately and energetically, impatient of details. Caring so little about money where one dear to him is concerned, it is impossible for Antonio to understand Shylock's obsession with money.

Shakespeare chose not to explain Antonio's attachment to Bassanio. Friendship between man and man is a powerful theme in many of Shakespeare's plays, and may have been an important element in his own life. The fact that Antonio acts so selflessly toward Bassanio because they are *friends* (rather than relatives) is an important part of the play's moral emphasis.

Materialism – a devotion to material needs and desires such as money – and hypocrisy are the evils of the play from Antonio's perspective. Against them stands a true friendship which is willing even to sacrifice the principle of not encouraging usury in order to borrow money for a friend.

The friendship between Antonio and Bassanio is of the kind discussed by Portia and Lorenzo – 'god-like amity' – which fortunately Portia understands. In the play, just as the Friend, Antonio, helps the Lover's plan at the outset, so the Lover, Portia, places the needs of the Friend above her own. At the end, Antonio, recognizing her worth, is willing to pledge his *soul* in a new sacramental union which links him with the lovers. Even then we may think that he is a little hasty about doing so.

Perhaps the strangest thing about Antonio is this impatience to hurry things along, even his own trial, as if he had seen it all before, or was awaiting some cataclysmic event. The contrast between his dynamic approach to business and his lack of insight into the motivation of others, as well as his general emotional shrinking may be a comment on the effect of a society intent on material pursuits on a sensitive man. Antonio's treatment of Shylock and his share in forming Shylock's own attitude to the Gentile society around him suggest that he is incapable of recognizing Shylock's humanity, his right to be considered as an individual. Thus, Antonio is not the hero of the play despite the admiration with which his friends regard him. He seems as isolated socially as Shylock, and his only role that of benevolent interference in the affairs of young people, those of Lorenzo and Jessica as well as of Bassanio.

Hatred: Shylock

The other main male character, Shylock, is a truly ambiguous figure, sometimes, in the past, played on the stage as if he were not more than an extremely cruel usurer. More often he is presented sympathetically as an outsider driven to an almost insane hatred by his ill-treatment within a society boasting Christian ideals, where the abduction of his daughter and the theft of his property was considered not only justifiable but a subject for laughter. Shylock's perspective is that of one who has been identified as an alien by the dominant social group and subjected to indignities unthinkable to an elderly man of some wealth in a European city. But Shylock has no social standing; as a Jew he could have none, except within his own ethnic religious group. His very clothes marked him out. Unlike Jessica, he could not be *assimilated*, to be made like the Christians, as a willing refugee. He performs an economic function which the community finds necessary. Since their religion forbids usury, the Christians need the Jews as usurers, for without ready money their society cannot survive. To Shylock the Christians are hypocrites and he persistently challenges their professed ideals.

From the very beginning, with the bald statement 'I hate him for he is a Christian', Shylock makes us focus on his motives. Such a remark would evoke a stock response from an audience with a racial stereotype in mind. But Shakespeare goes on to show how unChristian the Christians can be, and how dangerous can be the hatred of those we disregard or ill-treat. For all Portia's courtesy and persuasiveness, Shylock remains adamant. The Christians in the play may be mystified, but any under-privileged group which has developed a political consciousness would understand Shylock perfectly. He uses his religion to justify a counter-ideology he has worked out to challenge that of the dominant group. He is not ashamed of the customs or clothes which identify him as an outsider. Prejudice does not recognize the worth of an individual and denies him a specific personality. Shylock manipulates this to his own advantage in his dealings with Antonio and Bassanio and later submerges his own character in the cruel stereotype which has been imposed on him by the myths and propaganda of the ruling class.

Shylock is not a good man. His emotional life has withered away even more than that of Antonio. Shakespeare provides some small hints that this may not always have been so, as in his lament over the loss of Leah's gift and his outburst on Christian husbands who prefer the company of their male friends to that of their wives. But whereas Antonio lavishes his affection upon a young man whom he treats almost like a son, Shylock has a daughter whom he appears to neglect and take for granted, as her words to Launcelot imply. His home life is empty and we cannot blame Jessica for seeking love and fulfilment in Belmont. Her sadness when she hears music and Lorenzo's explanation of it suggests that she has been starved of affection as well as beauty.

Shylock is sustained by hatred but he demands that we share his outlook, at least partially, and for the time he is present before us. He begins as a creature of the original audience's preconceptions but overturns them by presenting other facets of his nature which reveal him as a unique and angry individual. His language, energetic and pungent with a sense of the real world, compels our attention; the Old Testament is a practical guide to him. He issues what is in effect a warning as to what might be expected from him in return for the treatment he has received:

Shall I bend low, and in a bondman's key,
With bated breath and whispering humbleness
Say this:
'Fair sir, you spat on me on Wednesday last;
You spurned me such a day; another time
You called me dog; and for these courtesies
I'll lend you thus much moneys'?

(Act 1, Scene 3, lines 119–25)

This is exactly what he proceeds to do. The speech embodies

259

his hatred of Antonio's ill-treatment, his incredulity at the friends' approach to him and the unlikelihood of a genuinely favourable response, expressed in deeply sarcastic tones. But their lack of interest in him as an individual as well as their preoccupation with their own plans prevent their taking him seriously. In Act 3, Scene 1 his revulsion against the Christian society around him is expressed in a sequence of questions which no one present cares to answer. The power of this speech lies in the fact that it is unanswerable. Again, in the trial scene, he asks questions about slavery which go unanswered. Shakespeare, like any great dramatist, asks the questions but provides no answers; instead, he directs our hearts and minds in the direction where answers may be found.

Shylock's very survival is made dependent upon his conversion at the end of the trial scene. Clearly, our views about this would differ from those of most of the Elizabethan audience. Shylock is obviously not the hero of the play, though a production may make him the dominant character. The question we must consider is: how much and what sort of a villain is he?

Love: Portia

If Shylock embodies much that is negative, Portia could perhaps be regarded as expressing the play's positive values. This view may turn out to be too simple in the end, but Portia is as capable of unselfish love as Antonio though her view of life is leavened with humour, sociability and a sense of gaiety. She is the most intelligent character in the play, as her conversation with Nerissa and her conduct in the courtroom reveal. Her attitude to life is unsentimental without being cynical, and her humour is sometimes almost sardonic. The ring plot she devises shows her grasp of the realities of life as well as her sense of humour. It performs the double function of binding the couple in an indissoluble bond of love to cancel the cruelty and materialism of the flesh bond, while ensuring that Bassanio becomes fully aware of his wife's wit and perceptiveness. Her hunger for love is demonstrated in the casket scene, but her sense of duty is so strong that she would weep but not detain Bassanio should he choose the wrong casket. She would not flinch from her duty as she sees it, however heavy and wearisome it may be:

> If I live to be as old as Sibylla, I will die as chaste as Diana, unless I be obtained by the manner of my father's will.
>
> (Act 1, Scene 2, lines 102–4)

This deep-going self-discipline and unsparing treatment of herself should prepare us for Portia's handling of Shylock in the trial scene. Once he has rejected her appeal for mercy, she pursues him with the full force of the letter of the law he had demanded. Our view of Portia is affected by how we answer the question 'did she know about the flaw in the bond or did it occur to her in the course of the action?' Her strength of character and generosity are admirable, but some critics complain of her treatment of Shylock, arguing that she plays him like a hooked fish and leads him to his ruin.

Antonio's friends

Bassanio is usually treated as though he were a minor character, and it is true that he emerges as a less vivid personality than Shylock, Antonio, or Portia. His courtesy and his affection for Antonio are evident, but his initial statement of his scheme to win Portia casts a shadow over the sincerity of his love, although a marriage based on economic interest was by no means unusual in high society then or now.

Of the minor characters, Lorenzo is the most attractive and his treatment of Jessica is usually portrayed in a tender and romantic fashion. He seems to be the only character with a genuine feeling for Venetian culture. Gratiano is thoroughly disagreeable, especially in his taunting of Shylock in the trial scene, though many in the original audience would have relished his gibes at the popular notion of a Puritan. Restrained by Bassanio and Portia, Gratiano is made socially acceptable, but his own personality, given a free rein, gives us a true idea of the Venetian society Shylock detested. His earthy vulgarity acts as a counterpart to Lorenzo's romantic outlook.

In *The Merchant of Venice* Shakespeare presents, by means of vividly realized characters, arresting scenes and powerful language, a series of conflicts – between love and money, romantic attachment and friendship, usury and generosity, justice and mercy, and so on. The settings in which these conflicts take place have the exotic interest of faraway places and the charm of fairy tale; but the conflicts themselves are as humanly relevant today as they were to Shakespeare's first audience.

The Merchant of Venice in performance

Patrick Stewart as Shylock in the RSC production at the Warehouse, 1979.

David Suchet as Shylock in the RSC production at Stratford, 1981.

Alec Guinness as Shylock and Richard Warwick as Antonio at
Chichester, 1984.

Ian McDiarmid as Shylock in the RSC production at Stratford, 1984.

The Casket Scene, RSC production at Stratford, 1984.

Questions

1 The four photographs on pages 263–6 present a sequence of Shylock's moods at key points in the play.
   (a) Where would you locate these points?
   (b) Describe Shylock's mood and emotions in each photograph.
2 (a) What does the physical appearance of each actor portraying Shylock add to the impact he makes upon us?
   (b) Which actor seems closest in physical presence to your own picture of Shylock?
3 (a) How do these Shylocks differ from each other in details of dress?

The Trial Scene, RSC production at Stratford, 1981.

    (b) Which costume do you prefer and why does it seem most
        appropriate to you?

4 Look at the photograph of the Casket Scene on page 267.
  What does the production gain from the size of the casket and
  its contents?

5 How does the photograph of the Casket Scene affect one's
  impression of the character of Arragon?

6 Look at the photographs above. Which Trial Scene do you
  prefer? Explain why.

7 What does the scene in the 1981 production gain or lose from
  the modern costumes?

8 What do the details of costume add, if anything, to the
  production of 1984?

9 Which grouping of the actors on stage do you prefer? Explain
  why.

The Trial Scene, RSC production at Stratford, 1984.

The Merchant of Venice today

Drama activities

Improvisation techniques are often used by professional actors to enable them to gain insights into the motives and feelings of the characters in a play. 'Translating' the basic situation of a scene into a present-day context helps to make the issues of the play more relevant to our own common concerns.

Borrowing   Act 1, Scene 2

1 Taking as your starting point Bassanio's need to ask Antonio for a further loan, improvise a scene in which you approach a sympathetic friend for a loan. You are uncomfortably aware that you have not repaid earlier borrowings.

2 Act 1, Scene 3
Since no one else is able to supply their needs, Antonio and Bassanio are forced to turn to Shylock the money-lender, who has no reason to like them. Using the above scene as a basis, improvise a scene in which you attempt to borrow or ask for help from someone who has every reason to dislike you. Focus on the reactions of the person who has it in his or her power to refuse this request for assistance.

Choosing a partner for love or friendship   Act 1, Scene 2

Very popular or attractive people often have a long line of would-be friends or suitors. Using Portia's amusing comments to Nerissa on the rival suitors as a starting point, improvise a scene in which someone discusses with a close friend the sincerity, qualities, and defects of those who seek his or her company. The discussion might begin with the popular person receiving a number of invitations to attend some social occasion.

Prejudice Act 1, Scene 3

Racial, religious, social or sexual prejudice can cause discrimination affecting social life, job prospects and, even worse, the self-esteem of individuals affected by it. Using the scene in which Shylock speaks out against his treatment by Antonio and his friends, improvise a scene in which someone tells those responsible how it feels to be the victim of prejudice. A possible starting point might be the fact that one can be quite acceptable in one kind of social situation and not in another – invited to be a member of a sports team, for example, but not to attend a team-member's birthday party. Another could be rejection as an applicant for a job because of religion, race, or gender. How does one fight these kinds of prejudices? (Swapping roles after a time can be very illuminating for the actors.)

Standing up for one's principles Act 1, Scene 3

Shylock refuses Bassanio's invitation to meet Antonio at a dinner party, on religious grounds. Improvise a scene where a person surprises a group organizing a social event by refusing to attend it, on the grounds that the customs or practices would, for example, offend his or her moral principles. The refusal could be based on disapproval of their food or alcohol, or because a sporting event is sponsored by cigarette manufacturers or an organization associated with particular political views. The group should counter the individual's criticism with reasoned arguments of their own.

Conflicting loyalties   Act 2, Scene 6

Jessica chooses to leave her father and her community in the Ghetto for ever. Choosing to reject one's family, community or culture, as Jessica does, must be very painful. In a multi-cultural society, young people must often choose nowadays to go against their family's traditions in seeking to live their own lives. They might wish to give up religious observances, to choose their own marriage partners, to continue their education, or simply, to emigrate. Devise a scene in which a boy or girl takes one of the above courses of action and tries to explain their decision to their family and friends.

Decision-making   Act 2, Scene 7 and Scene 9

In these scenes, Morocco's and Arragon's choice of a casket will make or break their fortunes. How they decide depends upon their estimations of themselves and upon the kinds of people that they are. Use your ingenuity to devise scenes in which someone has to choose between two or three possible courses of action and makes what is likely to be the wrong choice out of egotism, or because he or she is blinded by a romantic or foolish view of the world.

Judging a dispute   Act 4, Scene 1

In the Trial Scene we are invited to share in the judgement of a case where justice, in a strictly legal sense, conflicts with mercy. (An intriguing fact is that each word is used exactly the same number of times – thirteen.) The trial is Antonio's but sentence is passed eventually on Shylock, the plaintiff. Has justice really been done? Antonio escapes on a legal technicality which a lawyer drawing up the original bond ought to have foreseen. Does Shylock receive mercy in place of the justice he demanded?

Is the Trial Scene merely a public justification of the punishment Shylock is to receive?

With imagination, a group of actors could rework this scene in a variety of interesting ways. 'Translating' the situation again, we are reminded that the necessity to 'judge' in other people's affairs is part of everyone's experience at some time – between warring younger brothers and sisters, for example. Making a fair decision is very difficult in family situations where objectivity may be impossible or, at the very least, unpopular.

Improvise a scene in which a person or a small group have to decide which of two parties in a dispute is in the right.

School can provide many examples of conflict. A form may be locked out of their room or base because damage has been done and the Head of Year must be the final judge of a conflict between staff and pupils with different perspectives on the matter. Should a pupil be suspended because his hairstyle or clothing offends his Head? The Chairman of Governors will consult different representatives on the governing body before coming to a decision. If teachers' strike action results indirectly in an injury to a pupil, who is to blame? The possibilities are endless for a drama group which enjoys this kind of activity but it does demand careful preparation of reasoned argument and a well controlled debate of topics which are controversial and current in the school, the community, and in society at large.

Priorities   Act 4, Scene 1 and Act 5

When Bassanio is asked for Portia's ring by the young lawyer who has saved Antonio's life, he is placed in a most embarrassing situation. Who has priority – the lawyer or the wife?

Improvise a scene in which someone has to decide where his or her real obligations lie. A starting point might be the decision to use money entrusted to you for a particular purpose to meet what seems to be the more urgent need of a friend. Or the breaking of a confidence in order to save someone else from

273

injustice. The decision must be justified after the event to the person most concerned or hurt by the action.

These drama activities are merely examples of how an interested and active group studying Shakespeare might approach some of the issues of the play.

Imaginative writing

A good deal of imaginative work based upon a close study of the play may be derived from a change of perspective upon the main events. We prove ourselves to be 'active readers' participating imaginatively in the writer's task by engaging our creative energies with his. Make up scenes based on the following events.

Multiple viewpoints

1 Gratiano tells Launcelot how the Trial went.
2 Launcelot writes a letter home telling his parents about his new life in Belmont.
3 Shylock is visited at his house by Tubal.
4 Portia informs Bellario of the successful outcome of the Trial.
and lastly, an outsider's view –
5 An English merchant on business in Venice writes home to inform his friends that one of their business acquaintances in Venice, Signior Antonio, has been tried for debt.

Speculations: the missing soliloquies

1 At the end of the play, as the happy couples enter Portia's home, Antonio lingers in the garden. He confides to the darkness the true reasons for his melancholy.
2 At night again, Shylock wanders on to the empty Rialto to make his final speech.

274

3 At her window, Jessica awaits the masquers who will carry her away from home for ever. She hears their music and utters her thoughts, as she fills a small casket with the jewels which belonged to her father and mother.

4 On his country estate, Lord Falconbridge explains to his father's portrait why he did not, after all, take part in the lottery for Portia of Belmont's hand.

5 In a great tent hung with tapestries, the Prince of Morocco tells the desert air his true feelings about his encounter with Fate in sophisticated Europe.

6 At the Spanish Court, the Prince of Arragon looks into a silver mirror, and prepares to tell the King how he lost the golden opportunity to win an heiress for himself and Spain.

Speculations: the missing characters

Construct a short scene involving these missing characters.

1 Young Shylock receives a turquoise ring from Leah.

2 Portia's father assisted by his cousin Bellario draws up his will.

3 Old Gobbo reports his visit to the city and the fate of her dish doves to his wife Margery.

4 One of Antonio's captains explains the delay in the argosy's return home to Venice which almost cost his master his life.

Study questions

1 What do you consider to be the major themes of *The Merchant of Venice*, and how are these made interesting to the audience?

2 How far, in your view, is Shylock a victim of the society in which he finds himself?

3 Do you find Portia a wholly admirable character?

4 How should the part of Antonio be performed in order to bring out those aspects of his character which you find interesting?

5 Who are the play's minor characters and what is their contribution to the play as a whole?

6 What light do the following relationships throw upon the play's main preoccupations: Shylock and Jessica; Lorenzo and Jessica; Portia and Nerissa; Bassanio and Gratiano?

7 Examine the use of two of the following dramatic devices: the three caskets; the rings given by Portia and Nerissa; the scene between Launcelot and Old Gobbo; the scene between Lorenzo and Jessica in the garden of Belmont.

8 Describe a production of the play which you have seen (on stage, film, TV or video) emphasizing those features of the production which you found most enlightening *or* of which you disapproved.

9 Bassanio is the third serious suitor for Portia's hand – three being a magical number. How lucky is he in winning her?

10 How *relevant*, if at all, is *The Merchant of Venice* to a present-day audience and how do you account for its continuing *popularity* with directors, actors and audiences?